Mobile
$4.50
April 15, 1978

THE POLICE DEPARTMENT PSYCHOLOGIST

THE POLICE DEPARTMENT PSYCHOLOGIST

By

MARTIN REISER, Ed. D.
Department Psychologist
Los Angeles Police Department

With a Foreword by

Edward M. Davis
Chief of Police
Los Angeles Police Department

CHARLES C THOMAS • PUBLISHER
Springfield • Illinois • U.S.A.

Published and Distributed Throughout the World by
CHARLES C THOMAS • PUBLISHER
Bannerstone House
301-327 East Lawrence Avenue, Springfield, Illinois, U.S.A.

This book is protected by copyright. No part of it
may be reproduced in any manner without written
permission from the publisher.

© *1972, by* CHARLES C THOMAS • PUBLISHER
ISBN 0-398-02483-9
Library of Congress Catalog Card Number: 74-190335

With THOMAS BOOKS careful attention is given to all details of manufacturing and design. It is the Publisher's desire to present books that are satisfactory as to their physical qualities and artistic possibilities and appropriate for their particular use. THOMAS BOOKS will be true to those laws of quality that assure a good name and good will.

Printed in the United States of America
R00-2

FOREWORD

DR. Martin Reiser has been an invaluable asset to the Los Angeles Police Department since his selection as Department Psychologist in 1968. His innovative approach to the concept of the in-house psychologist has reinforced our original belief that such an idea could and would work. Dr. Reiser provides his fellow behavioral scientists with a look at what they might face if they undertook a similar task. However, his book is not limited to his specialty alone. The police manager might well wish to read it for his own purposes.

Edward M. Davis

PREFACE

THIS book represents one person's perception of what is involved in the unique and challenging role of police psychologist. Its main purpose is to explicate some of the dimensions of this fascinating position for psychologists, police administrators, and educators. This is done with the expectation that in the future the psychologist (behavioral scientist) will be less of a rare bird in the police profession.

ACKNOWLEDGMENTS

I GRATEFULLY acknowledge the cooperation and support of my many colleagues in the Los Angeles Police Department. To date, everyone with whom I have had contact has been genuinely interested in helping me in my task.

Because I have worked closely on a day-to-day basis with several capable and congenial colleagues in the Personnel and Training Bureau, without whose assistance I couldn't adequately function, I would like to thank Assistant Chief Daryl F. Gates, Deputy Chief Dale H. Speck, Commander Vernon L. Hoy, Commander George E. Beck, and Lieutenant Charles E. Brennan.

My wife, Enid, deserves special credit and appreciation for her unwavering encouragement and willingness to act as my amanuensis.

Permission has been granted by Charles C Thomas, Publisher, to quote from several articles in the journal POLICE: "The Police Department Psychologist," January-February, 1970, pp. 24-26; "The Police Psychologist as Consultant", January-February, 1971, pp. 58-60; "Psychological Research in an Urban Police Department."

The International Association of Chiefs of Police has permitted quoting from an article, "A Psychologist's View of the Badge", POLICE CHIEF, September, 1970, pp. 24-26.

CONTENTS

	Page
Foreword — Edward M. Davis	v
Preface	vii
Acknowledgments	xi

Chapter

1. CHOOSING THE RIGHT MAN 3
   Rationale for an In-house Psychologist
   Professional and Personal Qualifications
   Selection Process
2. GETTING PLUGGED INTO THE SYSTEM 7
   Orientation and Familiarization
   Public Relations Activities
3. DEVELOPING THE PSYCHOLOGIST'S ROLE 12
   Status
   Lines of Communication
   Line-Staff Questions
   Coordination of Behavioral Science Efforts
4. PROVIDING DIRECT SERVICES 16
   Personal Counseling Approaches
   Diagnosis and Evaluation
   Through-Channels Referral
   Community Resources
   Problems of Policemen
   A Psychologist's View of the Badge
5. THE SELECTION AND CAREER GUIDANCE
   OF POLICEMEN 27
   Job Requirements and Personal Qualifications
   Testing and Evaluation Procedures
   Psychological Problems of Selection
   Career Guidance

6. INVOLVEMENT IN TRAINING PROGRAMS 33
   Psychologist As Teacher and Consultant
   Recruit Training Inputs
      Human Relations Training
      Mentally Ill – Family Disputes
      Self-Image and Personal Problems
   Middle Management Inputs
      Problems of the Man in the Middle
      The Good Administrator
      Personal Relationships and the Counseling Role
   Top Management Inputs
      Symbolic Authority Problems
      Communication Difficulties
      Executive Stresses
7. THE POLICE PSYCHOLOGIST AS CONSULTANT 47
   Identifying Problems in the System
   Change Agent Role
8. SPECIALIZED CONSULTATION
   AND TROUBLESHOOTING 51
   Community Relations
   Homicides
   Vice
   Intelligence
   Internal Affairs
   On-the-Scene Assistance
9. THE RESEARCH ROLE 56
   Liaison with Other Professionals
   Assessing In-House Research Needs
   Developing and Implementing Research
   Anatomy of a Research Project
   Some Problems in the Research Area
10. SOME PROBLEMS AND DILEMMAS
    – ORGANIZATIONAL AND PERSONAL 65
    Confidentiality
    Service Versus Staff Conflicts
    Maintaining Professional Objectivity and Identity

The "Headshrinker" Versus the "Cop"
The Unconsultant
11. PROFESSIONAL GROWTH 70
12. THE FUTURE 72
    Some Desirable Directions
        And Developments

Appendix

I. SOME TYPICAL PROJECTS AND REQUESTS
    OF DEPARTMENT PSYCHOLOGISTS 75
II. HUMAN RELATIONS HANDBOOK
    FOR POLICE OFFICERS (SAMPLE FORMAT) 77
III. OUTLINE OF A RESEARCH PROJECT 89
IV. MARITAL SURVEY (A SAMPLE) 101

Additional Bibliography 107
Author Index 111
Subject Index 114

THE POLICE DEPARTMENT PSYCHOLOGIST

Chapter 1

CHOOSING THE RIGHT MAN

RATIONALE FOR AN IN-HOUSE PSYCHOLOGIST

FROM the Wickersham Commission report of 1931, to the President's Law Enforcement Commission reports of 1967, the concepts of professionalization of police and increased emphasis on service functions remain consistent. The old requirements that policemen have brawn rather than brains has significantly changed. Police officers now spend a larger proportion of their time helping people rather than arresting them. This requires an intelligent, sensitive and educated professional who can work competently with a wide variety of people in an often hostile environment.

The increased movement of police work toward the helping professions has highlighted the importance of interpersonal skills, psychological astuteness, and emotional control. Although hardware is still important in police work, it is now widely recognized that a human relations armamentarium is primary. In this regard, the behavioral science expert has a vital role to play. Since almost all of the areas of police functioning today have interpersonal underpinnings, the psychologist in the police department can make important contributions to selection, training, programming, career development, research, management consultation, and direct services to department personnel.

In many ways, a full-time, in-house psychologist is preferable to the part-time consultant, who has been the usual resource in the past. Working within the organization, the in-house psychologist will get to know the organizational structure and dynamics much more intimately and pragmatically. Since organizations are basically only people, relationships can be developed within the department which will enable the in-house psychologist to be perceived and accepted in such a way that he can accomplish things the "outsider" consultant can't possibly do. In this connection, police administrators are consciously aware of the psychological parameters involved in much police work and the forward-looking executives are willing and sometimes eager to utilize behavioral science experts more.

PROFESSIONAL AND PERSONAL QUALIFICATIONS

Ideally, the police psychologist should be a senior person with a relatively wide background of varied experiences to provide a base from which to adapt and develop. Skills and expertise in the areas of clinical, research, community, industrial and in individual and group therapy are important. However, because there are no explicit job requirements or specifications for the police psychologist's role, it is almost impossible to dogmatically state professional prerequisites.

Beyond a broad base of experience and professional maturity, the personal characteristics of the individual who will function in the police psychologist's role are most important. Emotional stability and personal flexibility are as essential here as they are in other professional occupations. The psychologist in police work has to be able to see himself and his own biases more directly and openly, particularly in the tendency to stereotype policemen. Also he needs to examine his unresolved conflicts in relation to authority figures. Additionally, the in-house psychologist needs a large storehouse of patience and a respectable frustration tolerance. He must also be aware and understand that evolution rather than revolution is the mode of change within most hierarchical institutions including police departments. He should be able to view himself as a kind of social change agent but one analagous to the business executive who changes the organization by updating and improving his company's operations and effectiveness.

Another important personal qualification is the ability to function at a very high ethical level in avoidance of power struggles, rivalry, contests and involvement in "family" fights.

The police psychologist will not infrequently find himself being attacked and ostracized by his own professional colleagues. There is a tendency to be stereotyped as "one of them." The blind spot of the stereotyper is in his unawareness of the fact that the police department psychologist is doing rather than talking and is realistically working at social change in the vanguard of society. The individual who is overly sensitive to attack or unable to identify with police department functions and goals would be poorly qualified for this position.

SELECTION PROCESS

If the psychologist is to function successfully within a police department, it is vital that he be selected with care, and that consideration be given to the particular needs of the department. Unlike current marriage practices, the wedding of psychologist to police work full-time should be preceded by mutual discussion, testing, evaluation and predecision counseling. It would be wise for the police department to utilize the services of a management consultation firm to participate in the preliminary evaluation and selection of applicants. However, the final decision should be made by the relevant group of police department administrators and colleagues who will be working most directly with the psychologist. In like fashion, the psychologist applicant in addition to being motivated to work in a police setting, should also closely assess the department, the position for which he is applying and the individuals with whom he will be working. Questions of compatibility, common goals, and open communications are important if one is to function positively in this environment. However, it should be kept in mind on both sides that much of what occurs after the psychologist is hired depends on a complex interaction of interests, needs, situations, personalities and functions to be developed.

BIBLIOGRAPHY

1. Reiser, M.: The police department psychologist. POLICE, pp. 24-26, January-February, 1970.
2. REPORT ON THE POLICE. National Commission on Law Observance and Enforcement. (Wickersham Commission). Washington, D. C., U. S. Government Printing Office, 1931.
3. TASK FORCE REPORT: THE POLICE. The President's Commission on

Law Enforcement and Administration of Justice. Washington, D. C., U. S. Government Printing Office, 1967.
4. THE CHALLENGE OF CRIME IN A FREE SOCIETY. The President's Commission on Law Enforcement and the Administration of Justice. Washington, D. C., U. S. Government Printing Office, 1967.

Chapter 2

GETTING PLUGGED INTO THE SYSTEM

ORIENTATION AND FAMILIARIZATION

ALTHOUGH it usually isn't feasible for a civilian employee to go through the entire recruit training program, it is essential for the newly hired psychologist to become familiar with what police work involves. This includes not only legal matters and procedural operations, but also an awareness of the various pressures and conflicts that are generated by the nature of the police function itself.

The psychologist should study the history of the particular police department within which he will be working. There are usually papers, articles and reports available in published form which will give him a general overview of the historical development of the department. He should also read the department procedural manual, training manuals and any other publications put out by the police department to acquaint him with the current practices, philosophies and procedures extant within the department. In the large police department with a central administrative building and outlying divisions, he should make it a point early in his tenure to visit each of the specialized and headquarters divisions including jail, property, scientific investigations, internal affairs, narcotics, vice, communications and others, in order to develop an overview of what types of specialized effort go into the police function. It is also helpful if he sits in as observer on oral selection boards for new recruits and on promotion boards in order to get a feel for the kind of standards and qualifications used in the selection process. This should yield some notion of the caliber of individuals working in the department. In this regard, considerable time should also be spent at the police academy sampling a wide variety of classes and discussing with the training staff the department's training philosophy and goals. The psychologist should make it a point to go to each geographic patrol division and introduce himself to the men at roll calls, giving a brief explanation of who he is and what his function will be, placing particular emphasis on the counseling role. He should arrange to sit in on some administrative meetings in order to get the flavor of higher level policy-making and philosophy, as well as to become a familiar figure to the top management of the department. In addition to learning about the operations of his particular department, the psychologist should keep an eye out for the kinds of problems he perceives as he is becoming oriented. This will allow him to reflect and to formulate suggestions, programs, research ideas and training modes as he begins to function in a more active fashion. One of the more important orientation experiences is riding on patrol in a police car. This should be done frequently during the initial orientation period, and continued as an ongoing activity at least once per month in order to keep in touch with field pressures and problems. It will also let the administrators and the men in the field know that he remains interested in them.

As in most other occupations, reading the literature constitutes a very necessary and important part of learning. In the field of police and law enforcement, there are a number of books, journals, articles and reports available which seem to be increasing at a geometric rate. As part of his continuing education, the psychologist should not only sample new books but also should make it a point to read regularly such journals, as POLICE, POLICE CHIEF and the JOURNAL OF CRIMINAL LAW, CRIMINOLOGY, AND LAW ENFORCEMENT. He should also persue some of the "classic" texts listed at the end of this chapter.

Learning is a lifetime process and it is therefore important that the psychologist not think that once he has finished his initial orientation and familiarization, he has done all that is necessary to learn about his police department's operations. There are usually so many activities going on within specialized divisions and at various command levels in the large police departments that it is incumbent upon the psychologist to be aware of these developments if only for his own general information.

PUBLIC RELATIONS ACTIVITIES

As a staff person, the police department psychologist will soon find himself involved in various aspects of public relations. These activities should begin in his own agency; that is, the psychologist has to make himself known and has to get to know others in order to become accepted and acknowledged as an "okay" person. An attitude of informality in dealing with colleagues is probably better than the maintenance of a forbidding or formal posture. As time goes along, part of the public relations effort might include writing a monthly column in the department magazine on relevant topics and preparing papers for convention presentation or journal publication. The psychologist might also write reports, grant requests and make suggestions for new programs or modifications of current ones.

Public relations activities with people outside the department typically consist of talks or panels at various school, church, business and other meetings in the community about psychological inputs and the psychologist's role in the police department. There may also be interviews with students who are writing term papers or are considering majoring in police science or some other subject related to police psychology. The psychologist may be asked to appear on a radio show or a television program to discuss some aspects of the police psychologist's role. He may be approached about a television series based on his job. Other frequent requests may include teaching at a local college or university, participation in specialized workshops and consulting with other police departments. In addition to all of this, the police psychologist will find himself in heated discussions with his colleagues at psychological meetings where he will be asked not only to explain his functioning, but also to justify policy operations, attitudes, brutality, and traffic citations.

Everyone has and is entitled to his biases to some degree – even the police psychologist. However, when working within a police department, the psychologist must come to terms with biases about policemen and authority figures and understand emotionally as well as intellectually the mechanisms of stereotyping and scapegoating. A brief anecdotal exerpt may be relevant here:

> The operator's cool female voice came over the police radio in measured tones, "12L20, a 211 silent at the liquor store," the address, "code 2." As Sergeant Uno finished writing the address down on his pad, he said, "That's practically around the corner. Hold tight, and when we get there, stay out of the way." Several seconds later, we screeched to a halt near the front of the liquor store. The sergeant alighted quickly, his hand resting on the butt of his pistol. At that moment two more police cars roared to a halt. I was standing off to the side protected by the open door of the car. I felt tense, scared, and pretty much out of my element. This was my first experience on routine patrol as the newly hired department psychologist of the Los Angeles Police Department. Luckily, in this particular incident, there was no shooting and things worked out with no one getting hurt. Since that first patrol experience in the Watts section of Los Angeles, I have gone on patrol once a month in different areas of the city and I find that my preexisting attitudes and perceptions have changed considerably.

Prior to being enlightened to the police role and being educated to the realities of police functions, I tended to have prejudices similar to those of numerous people including many of my professional colleagues. I was also prone to labeling and to generalizing about policemen rather than maintaining what I considered my usual scientific objectivity, that is, looking at each person as an individual and considering all of the variables unique to the situation before constructing hypotheses or arriving at conclusions. Contrary to the stereotype of the policeman being unintelligent, sadistic, anti-social and latently psychopathic, I found that policemen are actually people (9).

BIBLIOGRAPHY

1. Banton, Michael: THE POLICEMAN IN THE COMMUNITY. New York, Basic Books, 1964.
2. Becker, Harold and Felkenes, George: LAW ENFORCEMENT – A SELECTED BIBLIOGRAPHY. Metuchen, Scarecrow, 1968.
3. Bordua, David (Ed.): THE POLICE: SIX SOCIOLOGICAL ESSAYS. New York, Wiley, 1967.
4. Chevigny, Paul: POLICE POWER. New York, Pantheon, 1969.
5. Clark, Ramsey: CRIME IN AMERICA. New York, Simon and Schuster, 1970.
6. LAW AND ORDER RECONSIDERED. Staff Report, National Commission on the Cause and Prevention of Violence Washington, D. C., U.

S. Government Printing Office, 1969.
7. Menninger, Karl: THE CRIME OF PUNISHMENT. New York, Viking, 1968.
8. Packer, Herbert: THE LIMITS OF CRIMINAL SANCTION. Stanford, Stanford University Press, 1968.
9. Reiser, Martin: A psychologist's view of the badge. POLICE CHIEF, pp. 24-26, September, 1970.
10. Reiss, Albert: STUDIES IN CRIME AND LAW ENFORCEMENT IN MAJOR METROPOLITAN AREAS, Vols. 1 and 2, Field Surveys III. Washington, D. C., U. S. Government Printing Office, 1967.
11. Smith, Bruce: POLICE SYSTEMS IN THE UNITED STATES. New York, Harper, 1960.
12. TO ESTABLISH JUSTICE, TO INSURE DOMESTIC TRANQUILITY. Final Report of the National Commission on the Cause and Prevention of Violence. Washington, D. C., U. S. Government Printing Office, 1969.
13. Turner, William: THE POLICE ESTABLISHMENT. New York, Putnam, 1968.
14. Wilson, James: VARIETIES OF POLICE BEHAVIOR. Cambridge, Harvard University Press, 1968.

Chapter 3

DEVELOPING THE PSYCHOLOGIST'S ROLE

STATUS

THE professional psychologist working within a police department has considerable prestige, but is also somewhat suspect at the same time. The title "doctor" tends to inspire awe and create an aura of omnipotence in regard to his imagined powers. Because he is perceived as a kind of mind reader, he is also felt to be potentially threatening and dangerous. By being natural, revealing his humanness, and remaining open and accessible, the psychologist can help to reduce these distortions to a more realistic size.

To be effective in his role, the psychologist must be plugged in near the top of the organization. Designing myriad new programs, suggesting innovative approaches and utilizing brilliant thinking will not be significant if his plans don't get implemented. By working closely with a top-level administrator on a day-to-day basis the psychologist is in a better status position to have his suggestions carefully evaluated and put into practice, and to exert meaningful influence up and down the organization structure. If the psychologist gets connected at lower levels within the organization, there is a tendency for him to get pigeonholed, with less likelihood that his ideas and suggestions will get very far. In addition to direct communications at upper echelons, the psychologist needs to be seen as an "in" member of the organization.

In his staff role the psychologist tends to be seen by members of the department as a specialist who should have instant answers to any psychological question in any area of human relations. These questions include personnel practices, morale within the organization, selection of policemen, evaluating bizarre psychotic behavior within an individual, answering questions about ESP and astrology and assisting in the development of a form to record sex offenses.

In effect, the police psychologist is a generalist who has expertise in many of the psychological specialties. He must not only be flexible and refrain from establishing rigid limits as to what his role encompasses, but he must be willing to take on the widest range of requests and needs for his services. As this process unfolds, he will find his role constantly developing and evolving rather than remaining fixed or sterile.

LINES OF COMMUNICATION

The psychologist needs lines of communication to the men on the street in addition to status within the police organization and access to the decision makers and managers at all levels. This should include first line supervisors and middle management staff. He should also keep himself informed about what is happening generally within the department to continually integrate feedback about the various systems as he sees them in operation. In order to obtain information from the various operating levels, he should visit different divisions, go out on patrol on a regular basis and talk informally to the patrol policeman. He should interview a sample of men resigning or retiring from the department in order to get feedback on conflict areas and problems existing within the organization This will also yield a sample of the kinds of attitudes and complaints held on termination which may or may not be valid or modifiable. It is important for the psychologist to attend administrative staff meetings on a regular basis in order to know in which directions the department will be going in the future and to contribute ideas and assist management in achieving those goals.

He should stay in touch with the families of policemen by writing articles in the department magazine or by having flyers or training bulletins distributed periodically so that his service function can be explained and a channel for communicating with him kept open.

The police psychologist also needs to stay in touch with other professionals working in the field, not only in police departments but also in related agencies. He should maintain contact with other behavioral science professionals in the community by attending meetings, conventions and workshops, by presenting papers, writing articles, etc. This will allow him to incorporate the best of what is available in his own field and also inform others of what he is doing for their enlightenment and assistance.

LINE- STAFF QUESTIONS

Because the police psychologist occupies a staff position within the police department, he will find himself pressured from time to time to assume line responsibilities and to make decisions which really are outside of his responsibility and function. Division commanders may call with a specific problem about a man or a situation and ask for a "professional" decision. However, the psychologist should gently but firmly remind the manager that his role is as evaluator, information provider and even option suggestor — that he isn't the one to make the actual decision. If the psychologist allows himself to be put in the role of line decision-maker, he will soon experience conflicts which could well sabotage his usefulness to the organization. In industrial settings some psychologists have made the transition from staff to line management because of their own needs and interest in this kind of role. However, this typically isn't feasible in police departments because of the legal differences between sworn and civilian personnel and the frequent requirement that managers come up through the sworn ranks.

COORDINATION OF BEHAVIORAL SCIENCE EFFORTS

As the in-house expert on psychological matters, the department psychologist should be given and should assume responsibility for the psychological programs and efforts withing the department. He should be coordinator of contacts from community behavioral scientists and liaison with psychologists from universities and mental health agencies. He should be the department's mental health representative at agency meetings and should be the contact person for various department programs and policies which have a direct bearing on psychological or mental health factors. In large police departments it is difficult to know all of what is going on at any one time at the various levels of operation. However, he should make himself available for consultation and for actual participation in these programs when it is requested of him so that he can help contribute to the high level of sophistication desired in the program area.

The department psychologist will find it useful to assemble a behavioral science resource committee consisting of psychologists, psychiatrists, sociologists, a lawyer, criminologist, statistician, human factors specialist, educational systems specialist, and others who may be willing to volunteer their time and expertise as consultants to him and to the police department in areas where they can provide specialized knowledge. The department psychologist should stay in close communication with the members of his committee and should coordinate activities to keep them interested and involved. An emblem of recognition such as a membership card would be helpful in cementing their identification with the police department.

BIBLIOGRAPHY

1. Ackhoff, Russell: A CONCEPT OF CORPORATE PLANNING. New York, Wiley, 1970.
2. Drucker, Peter: THE AGE OF DISCONTINUITY. New York, Harper, 1968.
3. Goffman, Irving: INTERACTION RITUAL. New York, Doubleday, 1967.
4. KNOWLEDGE INTO ACTION: IMPROVING THE USE OF THE NATION'S SOCIAL SCIENCES. National Science Foundation. Washington, D. C., Government Printing Office, 1969.
5. Matson, Floyd and Montague, Ashley (Eds.): THE HUMAN DIALOGUE. New York, The Free Press, 1967.
6. Odiorne, George: PERSONNEL POLICY: ISSUES AND PRACTICES. Columbus, Ohio, Merrill, 1963.
7. Sayles, Leonard and Strauss, George: HUMAN BEHAVIOR IN ORGANIZATIONS. Englewood, Prentice-Hall, 1966.
8. Von Bertalanffy, Ludwig: GENERAL SYSTEM THEORY. New York, Braziller, 1968.
9. Watzlawick, Paul, et al.: PRAGMATIC OF HUMAN COMMUNICATION. New York, Norton, 1967.

Chapter 4

PROVIDING DIRECT SERVICES

PERSONAL COUNSELING APPROACHES

COUNSELING and psychotherapy usually occupy a significant portion of the police psychologist's time. As the in-house psychological expert, he provides counseling and consultation for police personnel and families in personal, marital, family, job-related and sundry other areas. The kinds of situations he can expect to encounter range from minor concerns about a child's developmental adequacy to severe emotional crises involving suicidal or homicidal potential. The counseling approaches typically utilized include individual counseling, conjoint marital counseling, family counseling which may include teenagers and younger children and group counseling for officers' wives or officers and wives in groups. Although most of the police psychologist's counseling and therapy is done in his office, there are times when he will need to visit someone at the hospital or at home for evaluation or therapy when office visits aren't possible. He will also find the telephone a valuable vehicle for consultation and other more informal approaches to problem solving. The psychologist will probably discover that most of his direct service time is spent in trying to assist with marital problems. Police work, a stress occupation, tends to influence symptomatology in marital areas in addition to eliciting somatic and other indicators of distress. The person coming for counseling voluntarily, where no criminal activity is involved, should clearly understand that this is off the record and a confidential relationship which will not be reported officially or have any bearing on his job status. If this is not done, the psychologist will find people avoiding him rather than seeking him out for assistance.

In addition to the usual verbal techniques of counseling, the psychologist will find it helpful to utilize certain theoretical notions, books and articles in quickly opening up a situation and helping to develop introspection, insight, and potential for understanding in individuals who may be resistant initially. In marital counseling, concepts such as constructive arguing (1), clarification of respective roles, child versus adult value systems and kind of self-image are very helpful. The notion of game playing (2) in interpersonal situations can also be used to advantage in making unconscious repetitive conflicts more vivid. Missildine's book (3) is often an aid in certain cases in explaining and normalizing reactions that are commonly experienced and exhibited by people seeking counseling. Numerous books are available in the area of sexuality which can also add useful information when sexual symptomatology in and out of marriage seems to be a primary concern of the individual seeking help (9).

DIAGNOSIS AND EVALUATION

Diagnosis and evaluation is another facet of the direct services responsibility of the police psychologist. He may be requested to evaluate an employee in terms of emotional status or ability to function on the job. Although this usually means a somewhat more formal diagnostic evaluation, the psychologist will also find himself assessing clients informally for his own enlightenment and making decisions about treatment approach and referral possibilities. Generally, the police psychologist's time is extremely limited. Therefore, he will most likely only be able to offer brief, crisis-oriented, time-limited counseling help. If his evaluation indicates that long-term psychotherapy is desirable for a particular individual or family, he will need to refer to an appropriate community agency or private practitioner for this service. However, the psychologist should keep in mind that the apparent seriousness or crisis nature of the situation is not necessarily an indication of the ease or difficulty with which it can be handled or of the prognosis. Because the police psychologist's time is usually severely limited, he is able to provide counseling only on a short-term basis with the understanding that after six or eight sessions there will likely be a referral outside.

THROUGH–CHANNELS REFERRAL

It is important when working within the police organization, to be trusted and to make clear the line between a confidential relationship which exists in a voluntary counseling situation as opposed to someone ordered to see the psychologist for diagnosis or clinical evaluation.

The psychologist wears two hats in his counseling role. In addition to serving as the mental health resource within the department, analagous to the private practitioner in the community, the department psychologist also has staff responsibilities. This means that a person may be referred to him through channels for evaluation and recommendations, with the explicit understanding that the psychologist will communicate his impressions and clinical judgements officially. It should be made clear at the outset to the individual being evaluated that the relationship is not a confidential one under these circumstances and that there will be feedback through channels. Supervisors and administrators should be advised that it is desirable whenever possible to have a man come in voluntarily in order to establish the counseling relationship as a helping, confidential one. However, in some cases where a man refuses to come in voluntarily, denies his problems, or otherwise refuses to accept a constructive approach, it seems proper for the supervisor or administrator to order the man to come in. This puts the transaction on a staff basis rather than on a confidential one. Even in these situations, the psychologist may be of assistance to the individual as well as serving the needs of the organization by keeping clear in his own mind his staff function on the one hand and his helping role on the other.

COMMUNITY RESOURCES

The police department psychologist should become knowledgeable early about available community referral resources. Ordinarily, there are publications by a welfare information service or other public agencies which catalog the community resources and their services. These should include information about fees, age limits, types of services rendered, hours and number of staff people. An additional tool for use by the policeman on the street is a small booklet outlining the mental health resources in his area so that he will become familiar with these aids on a first-hand basis and be better able to assist citizens when this kind of referral would be of help. Typically, the mental health network in most communities includes family service agencies, mental health clinics sponsored by the county department of mental health and state and local hospitals with inpatient and outpatient mental health treatment centers. The department psychologist should become familiar with legal resources in the area including referral for bankruptcy, Chapter 13 situations, problems of pregnancy, school placements and child welfare services.

PROBLEMS OF POLICEMEN

What are some of the common problems of men in police work? There are probably two main categories. One is the usual range of emotional states and problems which occur in people regardless of occupational status or group identification. These include problems related to personality development and traumatic situations, running the gamut from normal through neurotic to character disturbances. The second category of problems is job-related. These are shaped in part by the occupational expectations and pressures on the individual. Police work is considered a stress occupation along with psychiatry, air traffic control work, space engineering and others. Excessive stress over prolonged periods takes its toll. There are often exacerbations of common emotional problems reflected in marital difficulty, psychosomatic disturbances, excess drinking, sexual acting-out, etc. It is important to keep in mind that these symptoms are not unique to men in a particular occupation, but are usually exaggerated by the additional tensions and stresses inherent in the job.

Regis Walther (13) of George Washington University has over a number of years researched the effects of occupational and institutional pressures influencing and shaping the individual. He points out that there is considerable data showing that different occupations tend to produce different occupational personalities.

Over a period of time, every profession develops a common set of beliefs, values or working styles which come to characterize members of that profession. The specific inputs that help to develop these characteristics are: the attraction of particular types of personalities to a profession; informal and formal selection process for entry; the formal professional training; and the reinforcement of the desired characteristics and behavior within the profession. Using the Job Interest and Measurement Technique (JAIM), Walther has outlined the occupational personality of policemen. The most pronounced characteristics he found were: valuing the standards of authority; an orientation toward mechanical or outdoor activities; competitiveness; self-assertiveness; and conservatism. He found that the identification policemen feel toward authority is toward the standards of authority and not the person. Perhaps this explains the phenomenon of men in police work who generate negative feelings of being misunderstood by the Chief and yet continue trying to maintain department and community standards as a separate value.

Niederhoffer says that the police system itself is the main factor in changing a man into a special type of authoritarian personality as required by the police role. As a result of the system shaping the officer, he feels justified and even righteous in using power and toughness to perform his duties. This orientation actually seems to result in part from the need for men in patrol work to deal with the public in situations which require the use of authority and firmness. Consequently, the patrol policeman tends to be the most authoritarian of the police specialists (6).

Skolnick feels that the two basic factors involved in police work are danger and authority. The fact that the policeman must be attentive to situations that are potentially dangerous and violent results in the policeman being a "suspicious" individual. Danger also has an alienating effect which tends to isolate the policeman socially from the citizens he regards as a possible source of danger. This feeling tends to get generalized to the larger community resulting in a feeling of social distance between policeman and most segments of the community (10).

A PSYCHOLOGIST'S VIEW OF THE BADGE

There are as many personality types and individual differences among a large population of policemen as among engineers, teachers, lawyers or psychologists. Since they are human, men in police work have feelings about their wives and children, about satisfaction on the job, about being liked or disliked by people with whom they are working and also about the future of the society in which they live. I found, as research studies indicate, that policemen by and large are above the norm in intelligence, have better than average emotional stability, like working with people in a service function and have a strong desire to contribute to the betterment of community life. As Karl Menninger points out, "I have no charges to make against the police as individuals. They do their jobs as they learn them. They are not themselves criminal any more (or any less) than the rest of us. I consider them just as good as I am and I know many of them to be truly superior individuals. What I would point out is that they are trying to do an impossibly difficult job. They are caught in an obsolete, ineffective, crime-breeding rather than crime-preventing system, which we have inherited. My charges are against the system not the people in it. The system is ours as much as theirs" (11).

With exposure to police work I found my perceptions changing in rather subtle and yet perceptible ways. Previously, I had had no interest in what people were doing as I drove down the street. Someone in an alley, a group of people pushing and shoving, loud crashing noises, and transactions in local stores were or small concern to me. However, from the perspective of policemen whose job it is to be aware of what is going on in the community, to detect and arrest criminals and to prevent crimes from happening if possible, I soon found myself paying attention to what people were doing. What was happening on a darkened street, altercations, the possibilities involved in someone driving without lights late at night and all of the myriad other things that a policeman must routinely pay attention to, became important to me. This could be labeled suspiciousness or even paranoia, but I think I would label it good reality testing, attention to the job, and earning one's pay.

It becomes apparent rather quickly as one is identified with the police as "one of them," that a whole set of attitudes comes into play which does not correlate too highly with the realities of the situation. Many people seem to react negatively toward the policeman in an almost automatic way. The man in uniform isn't seen as an individual but as an amorphous symbol. This raises many questions about the dynamics underlying the role and functions of the policeman as perceived by the citizens in the community.

Many of the explanations for reactions to policemen involve socioeconomic, political, ethnic and interpersonal factors. For example, Doig says, "The police are also the immediate representatives of the broader system of law enforcement and criminal justice and they inevitably are associated with the weaknesses in that system. More generally, the police (together with the educational and welfare systems) are, for the ghetto resident, the visible and direct symbols of a government and a social system that often seems unjust and oppressive. Consequently, the attitude and behavior of the police officers have brought ramifications regarding the ghetto dwellers' perceptions of the government and society, and regarding such specific and urgent questions as the prospects for widespread violence in urban areas" (3).

The police are accused of being conservative and of not being agents of social change. At the same time, we admonish the police to uphold the letter of the law as it is written and to apply it equally to all people. The fact that the written law is usually about twenty-five years behind social behavior creates a disparity for which the police tend to be blamed. Police are basically governed by statute and yet have to deal with the variations in practice. So we create the dilemma of placing the police in the role of keeping the status quo as it is written in law and then expecting the police to exercise discretion in circumventing those statutes considered archaic or unenforceable. Thus, the police role is by mandate conservative and law-upholding, attempting to maintain an outdated status quo. This places the policeman in the untenable position between the forces pushing for social change and those who want to severely punish anyone who "steps out of line."

What about some of the other psychological factors which help determine feelings and attitudes toward policemen? Historically, people have been in conflict over power and status. Why do we seem to need a pecking order to survive in group living? One reason is mentioned by Storr. "Aggression is a drive as innate, as natural, and as powerful as sex and the theory that aggression is nothing but a response to frustration is no longer tenable in the light of biological research" (12).

Sovereign rulers used the mace as the emblem of authority and the teacher in the old school house used the birch rod for that purpose. Today it may be the Bigelow on the floor, the key to the executive washroom, or a badge and a gun. In any case, the conflict around authority, of who is in charge, and of territorial rights are as active today as ever. Over time we have been able to evolve in a minute way from acting-out of impulses to partial symbolic expression of them. In the conflict over autonomy versus dependency, questions of power and authority are central, and along with dependency there is underlying resentment, anger and rage.

During our early development we are largely influenced by the surrounding environment. Particularly important is the harshness or lovingness of the significant people in our lives. At certain points very early we begin to internalize some of these external environmental influences and take them for our own. But because the early perceptual and cognitive apparatus is only partially developed, there tends to be large distortions and misperceptions of what is assimilated. Thus the early conscience, which is the internal representation of environmental taboos and prohibitions, is frequently more harsh and atavistic than were the original external sources This vengeful conscience is typical for an early developmental level but it should be softened and modified by subsequent life experiences and the strengthening of one's self-image. However, in varying degrees some of this archaic conscience lingers on — an anachronism.

How do we deal with this punishing avenger inside of us? One defense is to gain distance from it. To do this we have to get rid of it by pushing it outside. A handy gimmick in this regard is the defense of projection. For this to work smoothly, we need a hook to hang it on. We need a suitable symbolic representative outside — an easily recognized authority figure who can fit the part, who might discover our wrongdoings and bring retribution on us. What better symbol of this feared punisher than the policeman who has a badge, club, gun, and wears the uniform of authority — a perfect scapegoat. This is quite a neat psychological trick. Now the thing to be avoided is out there. We can run away from it, fight it, disdain it, heap abuse on it, and through it all we can feel guiltless and even self-righteous.

The uncomfortable feelings that were internal before can now be attributed to our feared authority representative — feelings of being observed, the fear of being detected, the pleasure in getting away with something illicit and above all, the tremendous relief from guilt and anxiety now that we no longer have this "policeman-authority" inside of us.

Obviously, problems of conscience are greater for some people than others. Those who have come to terms with their internal conflicts can partially identify with the aggressor and so feel equal to and able to cope with authority and criticism. Those who have not been able to resolve this conflict to any significant degree reveal their distress by way of exaggerated reactions to authority and an intense need to utilize an external symbol as scapegoat. Along with policemen, other minority groups who have served in this capacity are "wops," "Polacks," "kikes," "niggers," and "spics."

In this sense, then, the policeman is serving above and beyond the call of duty. He makes himself available as a perfect stereotype, an object to butt up against and gain distance from in assisting those of us who are still struggling with this internal conflict over dependency, autonomy and authority. Skolnick has observed, "The policeman in America is overworked, undertrained, underpaid and undereducated. His job, moreover, is increasingly difficult, forcing him into the almost impossible position of repressing deeply felt demands for social and political change. In this role he is unappreciated and at times despised" (11). Much of the behavior of delinquents, criminals and adolescents becomes more understandable in light of the unconscious mechanism of complementary projection in their attempt to cope with the dependency-autonomy problem. I don't think the conflict over authority can be resolved very easily using superficial approaches. I would guess that the interventions having the most impact would be those influencing early child development, family life and education processes from birth through ages seven or eight. It is really a problem of larger society involving many social and ecological factors in the tremendous complex of interacting subsystems. Wilson touches on this aspect in regard to the relationship of police to the community. "Policy implications of this argument are clear though gloomy. Substantial and lasting improvements in police-community relations are not likely until, and unless, there is a substantial and lasting change in the class composition of the central city population, i.e. until the street-crime rate and the incidence of public disorder in the central cities becomes closer to that in the middle-class suburbs. Only then will it be possible to reduce substantially the police-community tension generated by practices like aggressive preventive patrol and the use of gross indicators such as race and apparent class as clues to criminal potential" (14). It is this awareness that has led to the recent emphasis on social systems approaches in relation to primary prevention rather than a piecemeal approach in looking for THE cause, but ignoring the total organism. I think we need to pay attention to internal as well as external variables.

BIBLIOGRAPHY

1. Bach, George: THE INTIMATE ENEMY. New York, Avon, 1968.
2. Berne, Eric: GAMES PEOPLE PLAY. New York, Grove, 1964.
3. Doig, Jameson W.: The police in a democratic society. PUBLIC ADMINISTRATION REVIEW, September-October, 1968, p. 394.
4. Menninger, Karl: THE CRIME OF PUNISHMENT. New York, Viking Press, 1968, p. 34.
5. Missildine, W. Hugh: YOUR INNER CHILD OF THE PAST. New York, Simon and Schuster, 1963.
6. Niederhoffer, Arthur: BEHIND THE SHIELD. New York, Doubleday, 1967.
7. Packer, Herbert: THE LIMITS OF CRIMINAL SANCTION. Stanford, Stanford University Press, 1968.
8. Reiser, Martin: On origins of hatred toward Negroes. In Levitas, G. B.

(Ed.): THE WORLD OF PSYCHOANALYSIS. New York, Braziller, 1965.
9. Reuben, David: EVERYTHING YOU ALWAYS WANTED TO KNOW ABOUT SEX. New York, McKay, 1970.
10. Skolnick, Jerome: JUSTICE WITHOUT TRIAL. New York, Wiley, 1966.
11. Skolnick, Jerome: THE POLITICS OF PROTEST – VIOLENT ASPECTS OF PROTEST AND CONFRONTATION. (A staff report to the National Commission on the Causes and Prevention of Violence). U. S. Government Printing Office, 1969, p. XXIV.
12. Storr, Anthony: HUMAN AGGRESSION. New York, Atheneum Press, 1968, p. 109.
13. Walther, Regis: JOB ANALYSIS AND INTEREST MEASUREMENT. Princeton, Educational Testing Service, 1964.
14. Wilson, James Q.: Dilemmas of police administration. PUBLIC ADMINISTRATION REVIEW, p. 410, September-October, 1968.
15. Wilson, James Q.: VARIETIES OF POLICE BEHAVIOR. Cambridge, Harvard University Press, 1968.

Chapter 5

THE SELECTION AND CAREER GUIDANCE OF POLICEMEN

JOB REQUIREMENTS AND PERSONAL QUALIFICATIONS

THE requirements for policemen in today's society have changed considerably from what they were in the past. A strong back and a weak mind are no longer sufficient. "Complexity inherent in the policing function dictates that officers possess a high degree of intelligence, education, tact, sound judgement, physical courage, emotional stability, impartiality and honesty" (21). The Task Force Report also points out that in addition to the fundamental requisites of education and above average intelligence for law enforcement personnel, emotional stability, common sense and integrity are also required as well as freedom from prejudices which might interfere with carrying out responsibilities.

Many of the studies on applicant and policemen populations have concluded that men in police work are generally above average in intelligence, are at the high end of the emotional stability scale, like to work with people in a helping way and are desirous of maintaining community standards (4, 7, 9, 12, 14, 23).

In general, the requirements for applicants to police work are similar to those needed for other professions. These include intelligence, emotional stability, a well-developed ethical sense, a desire for continued self-education and improvement, and a basic identification as a professional. This type of identity emphasizes personal and human qualities which is congruent with the fact that the policeman's work is largely a people-oriented, helping occupation in today's society.

Blum (4) is of the opinion that police administrators are the best ones to establish performance criteria. Factors such as the availability of applicants, their quality, the cost and disruption resulting from inefficiency, misconduct, terminations and related problems will help determine the cutting scores which will need continuous revision based on conditions in the job market, the department's particular requirements and feedback from the selection process itself.

TESTING AND EVALUATION PROCEDURES

A large number of police departments today utilize psychological testing as well as civil service tests and other means of screening applicants for the police occupation. Since 1952 the Los Angeles Police Department has had a consultant psychiatrist doing the psychological and psychiatric screening of police applicants. The overall screening procedure involves a written civil service test, a complete physical examination, an oral board consisting of a sergeant and two businessmen from the community, a background investigation conducted by trained investigators, psychological testing including the Minnesota Multiphasic Personality Inventory, the Group Rorschach and a Tree Drawing and a brief psychiatric interview. All of this information is then put together to decide whether or not a particular applicant is to be disqualified on psychiatric grounds. There is no attempt to select a particular type of individual best suited to police work. Rather the task has been to weed out those who are patently unsuitable by virtue of emotional or character disturbances. In those few borderline instances where a judgement is difficult to make, the candidate may be admitted with a note to the training division to further evaluate him during the five-month training program. Between 1953 and 1957, of the 760 applicants evaluated, 11.3 percent were rejected for not meeting the psychiatric standards for the police department (18, 19).

It is now widely recognized that a comprehensive test battery as part of the selection process has advantages in allowing better screening. Several comprehensive research studies have been done in this area. A recent one way done on the Chicago Police Department (3) and another is currently ongoing in the Los Angeles Police Department. The L.A.P.D. study is designed to determine if there is an optimal I.Q. for police officers and to establish predictors of success in police work using the psychological test battery approach. It is believed that some psychological standard measures such as the California Test of Mental Maturity, the MMPI, the California Psychological Inventory and a personal interview can aid significantly in weeding out the obviously unfit.

On the national level the International Association of Chiefs of Police is currently developing a nationwide registry of policemen which would allow for lateral transfer from one police department to another. This would necessitate setting up criteria and standards on a national basis as well as developing testing programs for selection, promotion and certification. This has been done in part by several other professions such as medicine, law and nursing. One of the benefits of the nationwide approach to standardization would be to program the bootstrapping of many of the smaller departments in poorer sections of the country. This would enable them to upgrade the quality of their police service in meeting these minimal standards. In addition to the registry there would be national training norms and standards which would help achieve more uniform training. This would affect police reactions and approaches in various parts of the country. If this attempt is successful, the police occupation will have made another step forward in becoming truly professional.

PSYCHOLOGICAL PROBLEMS OF SELECTION

How explicit should the selective criteria be for police officers? Should the same criteria be established in police departments of differing size in dissimilar communities with different expectations, philosophies and problems? Or should these criteria be tailored to the individual police department and the community it serves? In California, the state has for many years established standards under the Peace Officers Standards and Training Commission which gives basic and advanced certificates to police officers completing the minimal training requirements at these levels of police work. This has been beneficial in may ways, but particularly in allowing the Los Angeles Police Department to admit lateral transfer men meeting L.A.P.D. requirements from other California police departments on the basis of these certifications. This has saved time, man-hours, money and redundant training efforts in permitting these men to take an abbreviated initial training program.

Another important question in screening is should men be selected in or out? Should the criteria established include those positive qualities that every applicant should have in order to become a successful policeman or should there merely be an exclusion of those obviously emotionally unstable or morally unfit to be police officers? Is there a minimum intelligence level in order to do complex police work, and are there certain personality characteristics that a man should have in this job? If so, what are they? If it is possible to delineate these criteria, what kinds of measures, psychological tests, oral interviews, and other guidelines should be used in evaluating these characteristics? What is the break-even point in cost effectiveness of an extensive comprehensive test battery versus little testing and evaluating? These are questions still crying for answers.

Another knotty problem today is that of recruitment and selection of policemen from minority ethnic groups. If these individuals can be attracted to police work, should there be differential scores in selecting them? Is it possible to develop so-called culture-free tests so that people from educationally deprived backgrounds will not be handicapped? Obviously, these questions are difficult ones and as yet there are no easy answers. However, with more adequate attention to such problems and with more research efforts in finding answers, they should not remain unanswerable.

CAREER GUIDANCE

There is a need in the police profession for more department-wide vocational guidance and career development programs. Each man should be evaluated individually with a vocational test battery to assess his particular strengths and weaknesses and to help him develop his potential more fully. By focusing on each individual's unique possibilities, motivation for self-improvement, promotion probability and potential for improving the system should also be increased. Additionally, it would benefit the police department by sharpening assignments to specialized jobs based more on a man's abilities than on secondary considerations. In time, this program would help the department grow as each individual member of the department is assisted in realizing his creative possibilities. Ideally, to accomplish this goal, there should be a vocational guidance and career development unit established within the psychological services division of the police department. This unit should function under the guidance of a professional vocational psychologist. It should program periodic retesting to determine what effects the organization has in shaping the individual, as well as to find out what happens to certain personal traits as a result of maturity, tension, experience, marital status, promotion, etc. The unit should develop a test profile on each man in the department which can be utilized for personnel selection, promotion and specialized assignments. This information should be updated on a regular basis in order to remain current and be useful.

BIBLIOGRAPHY

1. Abbatiello, A.: A STUDY OF POLICE CANDIDATE SELECTION. Presented at the American Psychological Association Convention, Washington, D. C. 1969.
2. Amir, Yehuda, et al.: Peer nominations as a predictor of multistage promotions in a ramified organization. JOURNAL OF APPLIED PSYCHOLOGY, 54:5, pp. 462-469, October, 1970.
3. Baehr, Melany, et al.: PSYCHOLOGICAL ASSESSMENT OF PATROLMEN QUALIFICATIONS IN RELATION TO FIELD PERFORMANCE. Washington, D. C., Law Enforcement Assistance Administration Project #046, November, 1968.
4. Blum, R.: POLICE SELECTION. Springfield, Thomas, 1964.
5. Due, Lloyd: PSYCHIATRIC AND PSYCHOLOGICAL SCREENING OF POLICE APPLICANTS TO AN URBAN DEPARTMENT: COMPUTER ANALYSIS OF 113 CASES. Mimeo, 1970.
6. Goldstein, Leo: PERSPECTIVES ON LAW ENFORCEMENT: CHARACTERISTICS OF POLICE APPLICANTS. Mimeo, Princeton, Educational Testing Service, June, 1970.
7. Gottesman, Jay: PERSONALITY PATTERNS OF URBAN POLICE APPLICANTS AS MEASURED BY THE MMPI. Hoboken, Stevens Institute of Technology, September, 1969.
8. Hankey, Richard: PERSONALITY CORRELATION IN A ROLE OF AUTHORITY: THE POLICE. Unpublished Doctoral Dissertation,

U.S.C., 1968.
9. Hogan Robert: A STUDY OF POLICE EFFECTIVENESS. Washington, D. C., Experimental Publication System, American Psychological Association. Ms. No. 195C, Issue #C, June, 1970.
10. Johansson, Charles: POLICEMEN AND RECRUITS — VOCATIONALLY RISKY, MECHANICAL AND MILITARY. Mimeo, 1969.
11. Levy, Ruth: SUMMARY OF INVESTIGATION OF A METHOD FOR IDENTIFICATION OF THE HIGH RISK POLICE APPLICANT. Mimeo, November, 1970.
12. Matarazzo, J. et al.: Characteristics of successful policemen and firemen applicants. JOURNAL OF APPLIED PSYCHOLOGY, 48:123-133, 1964.
13. McManus, George, et al.: POLICE TRAINING AND PERFORMANCE STUDY. Washington, D. C., Law Enforcement Assistance Administration, December, 1969.
14. Mills, Robert B.: Use of diagnostic small groups in police recruit selection. JOURNAL OF CRIMINAL LAW, CRIMINOLOGY AND POLICE SCIENCE, 60:2 p.238, June 1969.
15. Mills, Robert B.et al.: Situational tests in metropolitan police, recruit selection. JOURNAL OF CRIMINAL LAW, CRIMONOLOGY AND POLICE SCIENCE, 57:1, pp. 99-106, 1966.
16. Molden, Jack: A survey of applicant testing practices by Konsoc municipal police department. POLICE, pp. 28-34, July-August, 1970.
17. Petersen, Margaret, et al.: PSYCHIATRIC SCREENING OF POLICEMEN. Presented at Midwest Meeting of the American Psychiatric Association, November 14, 1968.
18. Rankin, James: Psychiatric screening of police recruits. PUBLIC PERSONNEL REVIEW, July, 1959.
19. Rankin, James: THE ECONOMIC ASPECTS OF POLICE SELECTION: THE ORAL BOARD. Presented at Traffic Institute, Northwestern University, January, 1967.
20. Sullivan, Eugene: Psychological testing for police officer selection. RHODE ISLAND CRIMINAL JUSTICE BULLETIN, II:3, 1970.
21. TASK FORCE REPORT: THE POLICE. The President's Commission on Law Enforcement and Administration of Justice, 1967.
22. Varsos, Milton: Police selection — some problems and procedures. ILLINOIS JUVENILE OFFICER, April, 1970, pp. 19-24.
23. Walther, Regis: THE PSYCHOLOGICAL DIMENSIONS OF WORK. Mimeo, 1969.
24. Walther, Regis, et al.: THE CONTRASTING OCCUPATIONAL CULTURES OF POLICEMEN AND SOCIAL WORKERS. Mimeo, 1969.

Chapter 6

INVOLVEMENT IN TRAINING PROGRAMS

PSYCHOLOGIST AS TEACHER AND CONSULTANT

THE police psychologist is usually asked to participate in training programs within the police department in at least two ways — first as a teacher and then as a consultant. As a teacher he may be asked to instruct recruit training classes on handling the mentally ill, human relations, authority relationships, criminal psychology and a variety of other psychological topics. He may also be requested to teach sergeants, lieutenants, captains and specialists about related topics such as counseling problems, juvenile delinquency or sex offenses. In his capacity as consultant, the psychologist is expected to have some practical know how and expertise about educational processes, teaching techniques, learning systems and technology. He is frequently consulted not only about the content of a particular training module, but also about the method of presentation and specific techniques to enhance learning. Although the teaching and consultant functions may appear different, there is actually much role similarity involved. By direct exposure to the classroom situation, the students, the problems of effective teaching and by acquiring direct feedback, the psychologist can better assist others in designing and implementing training programs when he is asked for consultation. He will usually be asked to participate in training programs from the recruit level up through the executive echelon.

RECRUIT TRAINING INPUTS

Human Relations Training

One of the highly relevant areas in police training today is that of human relations. In addition to didactic course work on how to get along with people, it is also useful for the police recruit and the experienced policeman to be exposed to experiences with more impact. These might include small group discussions, confrontation situations, role playing, films, video tape feedback, case reports and critical incident techniques.

In the Los Angeles Police Department, a consultant psychologist has assisted in establishing the human relations training for recruits utilizing the small encounter group approach. Rather than bringing in outside professionals to be group leaders, it was felt it would be more effective if competent policemen were trained as group leaders. The small encounter group under the guidance of an experienced police group leader discusses key issues such as the role of the policeman in today's community, feelings about various minority groups, personal motives and feelings about policemen and police work, reactions to provocation and abuse, feelings about violent behavior and punishment, and ways of dealing with particularly difficult situations on the street. In addition to the series of small group discussions, there is also a community orientation visit where the recruits spend an afternoon in a minority area talking with and having lunch in the homes of local residents. This experience affords them a brief but vivid glimpse into the problems, opinions and life styles of individuals living in a particular environmental setting. It also helps minimize stereotyping on both sides. Often, the community residents come to view the young recruits as human beings rather than as symbols.

Another helpful tool is a handbook for policemen which spells out in detail official department attitudes and policies toward citizens on the street in accomplishing the police task. The manual should be used as a guide in recruit training and for inservice and follow-up training at regular intervals as well as for divisional roll call training. Over a period of time, this will help everyone to become very familiar with and reinforce those basic principles of human relations which the department feels are crucial to its successful functioning.

There have been numerous innovative and some not so unique programs developed around the country in the area of human relations. A number of them involve sensitivity training approaches. Others involve community rap sessions, police aides and a variety of other approaches. The Los Angeles Police Department recently implemented the Basic Car Plan. This approach assigns a team of nine officers and their patrol car to a particular turf in their division. In addition to assuming territorial responsibility for their area, the officers meet monthly with their community residents. They get to know many of the people and the citizens get acquainted with their policemen as individuals. Common problems are discussed and bridges of understanding are established and widened.

One of the problems in the past has been that recruits are taught ideal attitudes and policies at the academy, but when assigned after training to a geographic division, they are told by older hands to forget that nonsense and to learn the way it's really done. This creates a gap and a conflict between what is actually done in practice and what is taught in theory. In order to overcome this problem a program has been set up to select and train senior policemen as training officers. They will be assigned to work with recruits in the field at various divisions and will also remain involved in training at the police academy, so that any differences between what is taught and what is practiced would be lessened by constant feedback on an ongoing basis. The training officer is compensated financially as well as with status in order to emphasize the prestigious nature of the assignment rather than having it perceived as an added burden.

Mentally Ill – Family Disputes

It seems desirable to have the recruit training on mentally ill, suicidal persons and family disputes taught jointly by a professional psychologist and an experienced police instructor. The team-teaching approach minimizes the downgrading of the opinions of an outside person, while complementing and reinforcing those experiences and viewpoints each professional contributes to the discussion. In addition to films, tapes and case histories, it would be useful to have recruits visit a mental health facility. Touring a state hospital or crisis unit of a general hospital and getting an explanation of general admission procedures and treatment practices will familiarize the policeman with these operations and facilitate later coordination of efforts. In this connection, liaison between the department and the local county department of mental health will provide inputs on the nature of the cooperative effort, lines of communication, and the roles and responsibilities of the policeman and the mental health professional. Some instruction about referrral resources within the community is necessary so that policemen who get involved in a situation with someone mentally ill, not involving arrest or commitment, can assist the citizen to get help on a voluntary basis. It is helpful if the department publishes a pamphlet on outside agencies and resources in the community to which the policeman can refer.

Although the Bard experiment on the New York Police Department (1) indicated that it was useful to train a special unit of policemen to handle family dispute situations, a survey on the Los Angeles Police Department indicated that it would be less economical there because of geographic spread, population density and differences in frequency of occurrence. However, it is desirable to have adequate training for all recruits on the problems and techniques of handling family disputes since these incidents occur frequently in police work. Instruction in this area should include not only background in general psychology but also specific techniques including a hierarchy of alternative responses available in each situation. In addition there should be an awareness of referral resources such as family service, legal, economic, vocational and medical aid which may alleviate primary problems in some family dispute cases.

Self-Image and Personal Problems

Policemen are human beings with problems like most other people. However, because of the need to maintain an image of strength and imperturbability, it is sometimes difficult for men in police work to admit to problems or to seek assistance for emotional difficulties which they can't handle. For this reason, it is important to have inputs in the training program to point out and to legitimize the notion that having problems, whether emotional or physical, is a universal human experience and does not imply decreased masculinity or impaired manhood. The emphasis should be on the problem-solving approach as an intelligent, adult approach. Resources within the department and within the community should be reviewed and phone numbers and names of the agency contact person listed for use in the event a problem comes up at some future time.

Another relevant topic that should be discussed in detail is the importance of self-image on one's success as a policeman and its relationship to the professional versus the personal role. The man who likes himself, feels he is worthwhile and valuable and is confident and secure inside is the one who is less likely to be manipulated into a fight or allow himself to be provoked by an insecure suspect on the street. The professional policeman is secure internally and can be more objective about what is happening around him even when he is personally involved. He is better able to distinguish which problems are his and which belong to the suspects or the citizens with whom he is dealing, and he does not tend to confuse the two very easily. When he is provoked by a hostile suspect who is trying to prove his uncertain manhood by a power contest, the professional police officer immediately says to himself, "This is not my problem, it is his problem. I know that I am a man, so I don't have to prove it to him." Consequently, he can go about his business in a more unruffled fashion, accomplishing what he has to. When he is verbally abused, the professional policeman is aware that names are not going to hurt him because he is confident of his own worth and masculinity. On the other hand, if he is physically attacked or abused, the professional knows that this is not acceptable and he takes prompt action to contain the attacking suspect with whatever minimum force is necessary.

Another problem that invariably comes up for discussion with recruit classes is that of the wives of policemen and their difficulties in adapting to their husbands' occupational roles. Unusual hours, overtime and involvement in dangerous situations all contribute to developing stresses and tensions not only in the policeman but also in his wife. As a result, police work is actually a stress occupation along with air traffic controlling, psychiatry, space engineering, etc. In these occupations there is a tendency for a higher marital conflict rate, a higher rate of psychosomatic illnesses and other indicators of stress. If the recruits and their wives are apprised of these hazards in advance, they have a better opportunity to develop adequate coping mechanisms and put things in perspective than if they are suddenly confronted by unusual symptoms. Discussion groups of officers' wives can be a useful vehicle for counseling in tackling problems from the wife's point of view.

MIDDLE MANAGEMENT INPUTS

Problems of the Man in the Middle

From the sergeant, first-line supervisor, to the division captain at the top of the middle management ranks, there are pressures from above and from below which result in stress, emotional reactions and at times the feeling of living in a pressure cooker. The middle manager is responsible to upper level management. He wants to make a good impression, appear competent, make the right decisions and run his operation in an efficient and creditable fashion. He also would like to be accepted and even liked a little by the men he is supervising while also feeling he is not out to get votes in a popularity contest. The middle manager is torn between the need to understand his subordinates as people, to empathize with them, to remember when he was in their shoes, while at the same time maintaining his responsibility to the organization and to his superiors for carrying out policy and the larger mission. This may involve discipline, evaluation of an individual which may be disagreeable to both parties and other tasks which can be perceived as distasteful. Some of the more recent studies on stress and the development of psychosomatic symptoms suggest that the man in the middle is more vulnerable than either the man at the bottom or at the top because he is a person in transition. He has the dilemma of needing to conform while retaining self-confidence and self-control, whereas the man on the bottom and the man on the top have recourse to other defenses and ways of coping. The first-line supervisor may also find it difficult to step back from the take-charge role usual for a line policeman and allow the street officers to take command of the work while he maintains his monitoring supervisory role.

The Good Administrator

The good administrator usually has achieved a balance between revealing his feelings and openness on the one had and directness, honesty and not beating around the bush on the other. He tries to see his men as human beings who do not have to be perfect to be effective. He deals with difficult situations as problems to be solved rather than as problems in personalities. He also sees part of his role as helping others to clarify their own feelings and to retain individuality by looking for alternative approaches to problems. He doesn't try to mold them in his own image. He invites questions, confrontation and discussion and feels comfortable with diversity rather than feeling personally attacked or insulted. In this regard he has considerable objectivity which allows him to ask himself the question, "Whose problem is this?" This permits him to maintain a balance between empathy and a professional stance. To reiterate, rather than seeking control over his subordinates in the organization, the good administrator seeks task effectiveness and accomplishment of the mission for the benefit of the police department and the community. He also believes in the concept of self-motivation and in participation of personnel at all levels rather than in a dictatorship which forces things on people. He understands that involvement means emotional investment and feeling included rather than being on the outside, and he encourages as much involvement as possible by members of the organization. The good middle-manager wants each of his men to continually improve his effectiveness which in turn is a compliment to his managerial ability. He doesn't react to efficiency or to someone doing an outstanding job as a threat to his own position. Instead, he feels that the more outstanding his people are, the better position this puts him in and the more it reflects credit on his own executive potential.

Personal Relationships and the Counseling Role

One of the frequent questions raised by sergeant school classes is that of personal relationships between the supervisor and his subordinates. Just how chummy or how aloof should the supervisor be and what does his role entail in this connection? The question is even more difficult when it involves the personal problems of subordinates as they relate to the supervisor's counseling role. In contrast to the notion that supervisors should not get involved in a man's personal problems or in counseling him, in the Los Angeles Police Department it is felt that a supervisor has a legitimate counseling role and that it is essential that he have some competence in this function. The supervisor should know his men as human beings and as individuals rather than solely as units to be deployed. He should know their characteristic ways of behaving and patterns of response so that should something unusual happen or a drastic change occur, he will be aware of it. First, the supervisor should know some of the common early warning signs of emotional upset in order to tune in on them and be of assistance. A few of the frequent, noticeable warning signs are: (a) drastic behavior change, withdrawal, emotional outbursts, chronic fatigue and irritability (b) chronic marriage or family problems (c) depression — talk of quitting work or committing suicide (d) excessive drinking — alcohol on breath often (e) sexual problems (f) excessive altercations (g) accident prone — physical or traffic accidents (h) physical complaints — headache, backache, stomach pains and others (i) feeling picked on and misunderstood (j) deterioration in work performance (k) loss of self-confidence or loss of interest in job (l) frequent short-term absences without justification (m) inability to get along with partners and others (n) financial problems and outside complaints to the department.

If the supervisor agrees that he has a legitimate counseling role with his men, he should be aware that successful counseling does not require advanced academic degrees. Interest in people, a sympathetic personality and character traits adaptable to this role are the essential ingredients. A supervisor realizes that his men will have problems whether he wants them to or not. Therefore, there is really no avoiding his involvement. The question is, how should this be done in the most effective way? A supervisor who has frequent contact and is in close touch with his men is in a good position to spot problems early. In addition to helping his men, he also has a responsibility to the department in maintaining their high level of functioning. A sergeant who spots a problem can be the first to help and can frequently prevent more serious problems from developing. By tuning in on the early warning signs he can intervene and make the proper referral early.

A question frequently asked is, how should intervention be done and what should be the initial approach? In general the sergeant should be direct and honest without phoniness or any attempt to seem like a professional counselor. The counseling should be done in a private, informal setting, perhaps over coffee, where other people are not present. An informal, relaxed atmosphere will contribute to the establishment of comfort and lessen the anxiety which will likely be present for both parties at the beginning. The supervisor should frankly admit he is aware of possible problems and explain why. If the existence of a problem is confirmed, he can then offer assistance openly without beating around the bush.

In spite of its apparent complexity and technical implications, the counseling process itself is rather simple. It consists of several key ingredients. The first is establishing rapport which involves an attitude of equality rather than paternalism with the counselee. An ingredient very difficult to master is listening carefully. By constructively hearing and showing an interest in what the other person is saying, the very act of listening is helpful. It gives ego support to the individual so that he no longer feels alone in shouldering his burdens. It also provides some ventilation of the problems which allows the individual to get things off his chest and not feel so loaded down. In addition, it may encourage the development of insight by providing a sounding board for the individual's problems. When this is done, things can be viewed much more objectively than when all tied up with confused feelings. The next step in the counseling process involves reflecting back and clarifying feelings for the individual. Pertinent open-ended questions are in order here to get more information. An atmosphere of interrogation or third degree needs to be avoided. After the problems have been explored and comprehended, the supervisor should be able to give a summary of what is involved in the situation as he sees it. A discussion of some alternative approaches to the problem should follow with the understanding that the individual being counseled is going to make the decision. He should not be told what to do as if he were a child, but should be helped to see that he is an adult who can make a decision, and there are roads open to him that he wasn't aware of before because he was emotionally involved.

Some of the things supervisors should avoid in the counseling role are first, postponing a confrontation or being hesitant and indirect which probably helps to build tension and magnifies the problem, and second, prejudging the person in the situation. A neutral attitude means an open mind. In addition, criticizing or moralizing will likely change the relationship and turn off the individual. Third, playing the mastermind shows an attitude of omnipotence and is actually an intellectual put-down. Fourth, guard against being too self-critical and fearful of getting involved. The supervisor should be award that even professional psychologists and psychiatrists make mistakes and are not perfect in their helping role, even after many years of experience. Five, don't react personally rather than objectively. The supervisor should keep in mind that although he should empathize, it is someone else's problem and not his that is being discussed. This is important if he is to be able to keep enough psychological distance to be of help.

What are the limits of this level of counseling and when should a referral be made? Generally speaking, the supervisor should limit his counseling to a few sessions and if sufficient resolution isn't achieved in that time, a referral should be made. He should refer long-standing problems of a chronic nature at the outset. He should have the feeling that some brief counseling in itself may help the individual, but he should avoid playing psychiatrist. This means not labeling the individual with some diagnostic put-down.

Referral should be made when there are suicidal or homicidal tendencies or psychotic behavior. When specialized help is needed with legal or finiancial problems, referral should be made early. If an evaluation of a person's emotional status is needed to determine whether he is in fact seriously disturbed, an immediate referral should be made for that. If after one to four sessions of counseling the problems still persist or are getting worse, referral is indicated. Whenever the supervisor feels he is getting out of his depth or is uncomfortable in his counseling role, he should also refer.

In making a referral he should explain to the individual the reason for the referral, and try to "sell" the referral. It sometimes helps to mention that getting help is neither unmanly nor a put-down, but rather like going to the dentist when you have a toothache. It is the intelligent thing to do. The referral should be on a voluntary basis whenever possible. However, in some cases when this is not possible, he should feel comfortable in making a mandatory, through-channels referral. This alternative may be necessary to help the individual. The supervisor can help get the person to the appointment by making the initial phone call. If he is interested, the supervisor may want to follow up the referral to find out if the appointment has been kept, what the current status is or to gain added information on how he might be of further assistance.

The police department should have a psychologist, psychiatrist or trained counseling person who can routinely be of assistance to policemen and immediate families. There should also be an established network of resources outside of the police department including community clinics, county agencies and private practice settings. Provisions for hospitalization for psychiatric or psychosomatic problems should be made. The supervisor should be familiar with the various community resources which are potentially useful. These are usually published by a welfare information service agency or county mental health agency and list the kinds of services, hours, fee schedules and phone numbers. Training in counseling and referral should be presented at the sergeants' school, or in smaller departments, in seminars which can usually be arranged with an outside consultant sitting in as instructor.

TOP MANAGEMENT INPUTS

Symbolic Authority Problems

The chief of police and assistant chiefs in a large police department will commonly find that some problems will arise as a result of their authority roles and have little or no personal basis.

These conflicts will likely have symbolic significance. That is, the chiefs represent authority, the establishment, "big daddy" and will be resented unconsciously on that basis alone by a significant number of individuals who haven't resolved their own conflicts in this area. It is not unusual for a considerable number of policemen to have some ambivalence toward the top man. They may be fiercely loyal on the one hand and yet be very angry and resentful of him on the other, sometimes having both feelings at the same time. This accounts for some of the rapid vacillations in feeling that may occur depending on the satisfaction or frustration of particular dependency needs within the organization at a point in time. When salaries are raised or when other basic needs are being met that can be attributed to the power structure, there is a tendency for feelings of loyalty or closeness to result. However, if there is some frustration in the ranks, feelings of being uncared for and misunderstood results. If an order comes down which is resented, a feeling of dislike and distance from the chief may result.

Communication Difficulties

Some of this can be ameliorated by developing an open communication system within the police department with communications going up and down freely. Although police departments are considered quasi-military organizations with channels, structure and hierarchy, it is possible nevertheless to arrange for relatively free information flow. This requires that those men at the top and at the bottom have contact with one another and exchange ideas and feedback information, as well as communicating to the next echelon only. Although it is difficult for top management people to make field visits frequently because of the press of work which keeps them in the office most of the time, it is important through occasional visits in the field to let the men see that top management is interested. It also provides an opportunity to get to know them as human beings and generate a feeling of closeness. In addition, regular use of closed circuit television would add to the process. It should also be possible for men from different divisions to sit down with the chiefs to discuss problems or gripes. Communication difficulties increase the griping and the likelihood of morale problems. Older men feel dissatisfied and disgruntled and talk more about resigning or retiring early in this situation.

Executive Stresses

Top management of the organization is frequently under much stress related to the executive function. The police executive is vitally interested in what his organization says, what it actually does and what the community believes it is doing. If these three areas are congruent, there is probably not too much static in the system. However, if there is a big disparity between the internal image of the department and the image in the community, there will be added conflict and stress for the executives in the organization. Additional stresses relate to organizational change versus resistance to change and maintaining the status quo. The executive also has those common tensions which are related to his own family, his marital situation and the satisfactions he is getting outside of his job. Training programs for top management should include seminars and modules on personal stresses, personal goals, self-evaluation, assessment of strengths and weaknesses and the need to maintain a balance in the various aspects of one's life.

Top management experiences considerable pressure from subordinates in the organization and from the community. Although the police department is a community agency, financed and supported by the community, there are frequent conflicts arising because of varying political, economic and social problems which exist in different parts of the community. This makes it difficult to satisfy everyone using only one set of principles or goals. It also causes top management to make hard choices between attempting to satisfy everybody unsuccessfully or aiming for some optimal ideal of law enforcement which will be accepted by the majority of the community.

BIBLIOGRAPHY

1. Bard, M.: TRAINING POLICE AS SPECIALISTS IN FAMILY CRISIS

INTERVENTION. Law Enforcement Assistance Administration, 1970.
2. Brandstatter, A. F. and Radelet, L. A.: POLICE AND COMMUNITY RELATIONS: A SOURCEBOOK. New York, Glencoe, 1968.
3. Briggs, L. J.: HANDBOOK OF PROCEDURES FOR THE DESIGN OF INSTRUCTION. American Institute for Research, 1970.
4. Briggs, L. J. et al.: INSTRUCTIONAL MEDIA. American Institute for Research, 1967.
5. Briggs, L. J.: SEQUENCING OF INSTRUCTION IN RELATION TO HIERARCHIES OF COMPETENCE. American Institute for Research, 1968.
6. Drucker, P.: MANAGING FOR RESULTS. New York, Harper, 1964.
7. Drucker, P.: THE EFFECTIVE EXECUTIVE. New York, Harper, 1966.
8. Dudycha, G. J.: PSYCHOLOGY FOR LAW ENFORCEMENT OFFICERS. Springfield, Thomas, 1970.
9. Epstein, C.: INTERGROUP RELATIONS FOR POLICE OFFICERS. Baltimore, Williams & Wilkins, 1962.
10. Gammage, A. Z.: POLICE TRAINING IN THE UNITED STATES. Springfield, Thomas, 1963.
11. Iannone, N.: SUPERVISION OF POLICE PERSONNEL. Englewood Cliffs, Prentice-Hall, 1970.
12. Levinson, H.: EMOTIONAL HEALTH IN THE WORLD OF WORK. New York, Harper, 1964.
13. Levinson, H.: EXECUTIVE STRESS. New York, Harper, 1970.
14. POLICE RESPONSE TO FAMILY DISPUTES: A Training Manual for Family Crisis Intervention. New York Police Department, 1969.
15. POLICE TRAINING. International Association of Chiefs of Police, Washington, D. C. 1966.
16. Siegel, A. et al.: PROFESSIONAL POLICE – HUMAN RELATIONS TRAINING. Springfield, Thomas, 1963.
17. Watson, N. A.: POLICE – COMMUNITY RELATIONS. International Association of Chiefs of Police, Washington, D. C. 1966.

Chapter 7

THE POLICE PSYCHOLOGIST AS CONSULTANT

IDENTIFYING PROBLEMS IN THE SYSTEM

WHAT are the dimensions of the police psychologist consultant function? Generally, he is available and on call to anyone in the department who requests his services. As Gilbert (3) has pointed out, the consultant's role in a process depends on the function the consultant is expected to perform. This will largely be determined by the kinds of problems that arise within the organization as will as the communication channels which are open. In practice the consultant finds himself shifting and modifying his frame of reference to accommodate the various requests for service. This leads to a spiral process of expansion of his perceived, legitimate role. The result is not only challenging but can be satisfying. One of the main problems related to the consultant's role within a large organization is that of identification. Is the consultant primarily a mental health specialist, a social change agent, an organization staff specialist, or an employee in a hierarchy? Into what niche does the consultant fit? Answers to these questions depend in part on the level at which he gets plugged in. It will determine how he sees himself and how he is seen by other members of the organization, particularly those in power. If the consultant feels he is adequately connected, has sufficent status and the power to have a decent percentage of his suggestions implemented, he tends to strengthen his identification with the organization. I think it is important that the consultant be connected near the top of the organization. This gives him input and feedback accessibility to those who have decision-making power. If the consultant gets connnected at lower levels within the organization, there is a tendency for him to get pigeonholed with little likelihood that his ideas will get a fair hearing and trial. In addition to communications at upper echelons, the consultant needs to be viewed as an "in" member of the organization. Levinson (5) has pointed out that there is a tendency for a distance to occur between the scientist-consultant and the managers in an organization. The managers sometimes tend to be somewhat fearful of the consultant and therefore will isolate him. This may partly reflect the administrator's unconscious fear of magical powers, of being usurped or brainwashed in some way. To avoid being sidetracked, the consultant must develop personal relationships within the organization. These personal contacts will reassure others that he need not be feared, does not have magical powers, and that he, too, is a rational, pragmatic person speaking the same language as others and having similar goals. To a large degree, success or lack of it hinges largely on the consultant's personal adaptability and to a lesser degree on his intellectual and scientific acumen. What are some of the other conflicts or problems that have come up in regard to the consultant's role? One conflict the consultant has to resolve is that of wearing two hats. On the one hand he is a staff member in the organization and on the other, he is a therapist trying to help an individual employee. Unless he can clearly balance the two roles for himself, ethical and practical problems can arise. The role he is filling should be made clear at the beginning of any transaction with an individual when he is acting primarily as a staff person. In the staff role, confidentiality is observed, but as a secondary responsibility to the needs of the organization. In the therapist role confidentiality is primary. For example, if a policeman is referred through channels to the psychologist for evaluation because it is thought he might be dangerous to himself or to others, the consultant has the responsibility to report his findings to the administration while at the same time trying to assist the individual as much as possible. However, the overriding responsibility is to the organization. This is analogous to the psychiatrist employed by the court to examine an arrestee.

Another potential conflict centers around loyalty. How much should one identify with the goals of the organization, and how much should one try to remain neutral or independent of these goals? My own feeling is that if the consultant is to be effective within the organization, he has to learn to function within the limits and towards the goals the organization has delineated. Implicit in this notion is the expectation that viable organizations are not static but are dynamically evolving. Unless he adopts this view, the consultant might soon find himself a rebel in conflict with the goals of his organization and colleagues and will likely be unsuccessful in what he is hoping to achieve. It is important that the outset that the consultant be able to accept the general principles of the organization within which he is working; otherwise the dissonance and frustration would surely build up and impede his functioning to a significant degree. In trying to communicate psychological approaches or concepts to police personnel, the consultant should avoid jargon or the typical intellectual approach. He cannot deal with the men as if they were patients rather than consultees. If he errs in this way, resistances will be encouraged and he will find his suggestions discounted and he himself not taken seriously. Some of the mutual distrust that exists between behavioral science professionals and police personnel relates to stereotyping tendencies on both sides. Familiarization and individual personal contact help dispel groundless fears much faster than lecturing, name-calling, or scapegoating.

CHANGE AGENT ROLE

As to whether the police consultant should be a change agent, I would answer yes and no. I would say no if the definition of change agent means being a revolutionary and a militant dissenter. I would say yes because the consultant functions as a change agent in much the same way that the forward-looking manager or administrator does. He tries to balance the demands of the society in which his organization has to function and the internal needs of the department to achieve common long-range goals. Perhaps there is also a vital balance in the relationship of social systems and community organizations (6). But whether one works in a police department, a university, a hospital or other hierarchical institution there is built-in resistance to rapid change. This suggests a premium on patience and the ability to work within the parameters of the system although it may seem tedious and frustrating (8).

In his consultant role the police psychologist should work on a day-to-day basis with an assistant or deputy chief in a large police department or with the chief in a smaller department. This will insure that his inputs can have significant bearing and impact on organizational functioning via the top administration. By helping the administrators clarify their relationships to the men and to the community, and by helping them establish and achieve their goals in a realistic fashion, the psychologist can provide a valuable service in his consultant role. His aid can be particularly significant in the areas of community relations, selection, morale, the informal communications network, and in specific problem-solving.

BIBLIOGRAPHY

1. Caplan, Gerald: THE THEORY AND PRACTICE OF MENTAL HEALTH CONSULTATION. New York, Basic Books, 1970.
2. Drucker, Peter: THE EFFECTIVE EXECUTIVE. New York, Harper, 1967.
3. Gilbert, Ruth: Functions of the consultant. TEACHER'S COLLEGE RECORD, 61:177-187, 1960.
4. Goffman, Irving: INTERACTION RITUAL. Garden City, Doubleday, 1967.
5. Levinson, Harry: EXECUTIVE STRESS. New York, Harper, 1970.
6. Menninger, Karl, et al.: THE VITAL BALANCE. New York, Viking, 1963.
7. Neff, Walter: WORK AND HUMAN BEHAVIOR. New York, Atherton, 1968.
8. Reiser, Martin: The police psychologist as consultant. POLICE, 15:58-60, January-February 1971.
9. Sayles, Leonard & Strauss, George: HUMAN BEHAVIOR IN ORGANIZATIONS. Englewood Cliffs, Prentice-Hall, 1966.

Chapter 8

SPECIALIZED CONSULTATION AND TROUBLESHOOTING

COMMUNITY RELATIONS

MOST large police departments have a specialized community relations unit whose full-time assignment is to stay in touch with what is happening in the various segments of the local community and to augment two-way communication between the citizens and the police department. This is not a public relations function in the sense of merely improving the department's image, but is intended to diminish negative feelings, unrealistic expectations and stereotypes that usually grow and become more exaggerated when mutual discussion and interaction are minimal.

On numerous occasions the department psychologist is apt to be consulted by the community relations specialist about specific problems that exist and to help define some alternative approaches. It is not unusual today for some bad feeling to develop within the police department between officers of various ethnic groups similar to what occurs in the larger community. The psychologist can help by using a small-group discussion approach with involved policemen so that the problem can be examined, feelings confronted, and possible solutions examined. The psychologist's familiarity with nonverbal communication and unconscious processes gives him an advantage over the nonpsychologist group leader who may overlook or misinterpret because he is focused on more conscious and obvious kinds of communication.

Another important way in which the psychologist can assist in the community relations effort is by helping to design surveys and sampling techniques to determine the actual feelings of various community members, not only in regard to policemen and the police department, but also in regard to larger social issues in which the police play a significant role. By assisting the community relations specialists in utilizing stratified random sample techniques, questionnaire design, item analysis, and interpretation of the results, the psychologist can contribute to better assessment of the actual state of affairs in the community. Topics surveyed would include grievances, tension and support among various ethnic groups which the police are serving.

The psychologist may be asked to design and implement a small encounter group for community relations personnel or administrators in order to help them become more sensitive to community groups, problems and positive approaches. These processes will be facilitated if he uses a work-oriented problem-solving approach and avoids the typical sensitivity training format which seems to generate a great deal of antipathy among many policemen.

HOMICIDES

The psychologist may find himself consulted by detectives of the homicide division in regard to a bizarre murder having obvious psychological underpinnings with a kind of logical meaning beneath the irrational surface appearances. By interpreting unconscious motivations as well as the conscious ones, he can help to make sense of an apparently senseless murder, sex crime or drug-involved case. In this regard, it is important that the psychologist do his homework before he attempts to give advice to the experienced homicide investigator. He should know something about the incidence of homicide in various socioeconomic, ethnic, age, sex and occupational groups. He should also be aware of the connections between suicidal and homicidal impulses, the unconscious significance of various weapons and the relationship of sex and aggression to development, education, socioeconomic level and situational factors.

VICE

Another common consultation situation is testifying in court as an expert witness on pornography for the vice division. In this case, the homework is familiarizing oneself with the case law on prurient interest, obscenity, community standards and redeeming social value, as well as research studies bearing on the effects of sexually stimulating material on children, adolescents and adults.

INTELLIGENCE

Detectives from intelligence division may request a behavior profile of a suspect under surveillance thought to be considering assassination or murder. Using the background information and other data that intelligence officers have compiled, the psychologist should be willing to made inferences and predictions that would be of assistance to these officers in protecting someone's life. This kind of assignment will likely take all of his clinical skills, knowledge of personality development and psychopathology plus a generous amount of informed speculation in arriving at some defensible probabilities.

INTERNAL AFFAIRS

The internal affairs division of the police department is that investigative unit which looks into charges against policemen, whether by citizens, other policemen or by the department itself. The question of emotional stability may be raised when an officer is accused of misconduct. This, then, brings in the psychologist for psychological assessment and consultation. In addition, there may be questions about the man's ability to function as a policeman in the community or perhaps an inside assignment, a recommendation of a leave of absence or hospital treatment. In a special situation, the internal affairs investigators may be interested in clearing a policeman who has been unjustly accused or who is being treated unfairly. They may then ask the psychologist's assistance in providing psychological information which can help reinstate the officer or clear him from previous charges. On some occasions this requires testifying as a witness at a Board of Rights hearing for the officer.

ON-THE-SCENE ASSISTANCE

Although it usually doesn't happen often, occasionally a request will be made for the police psychologist to come to the scene of an incident involving a policeman, family member or citizen who may be threatening suicide or be barricaded. However, in most situations involving mentally disturbed individuals, policemen are usually able to handle the situation adequately without the presence of a mental health expert. Another type of on-the-scene assistance which is of dramatic interest to the psychologist, but which may be of limited help to the officers, is the campus disturbance or crowd confrontation situation. In this regard, the psychologist can probably help most by talking to the police administrators about the stresses policemen develop when involved in long hours of confronting or controlling crowds that are hostile, provocative or assaultive. In this connection, a range of adjunctive techniques including humor, music and singing should be considered (4).

BIBLIOGRAPHY

1. Arther, Richard: THE SCIENTIFIC INVESTIGATOR. Springfield, Thomas, 1965.
2. Camps, F. E.: THE INVESTIGATION OF MURDER. Michael Joseph, 1966.
3. Clor, Henry.: OBSCENITY AND PUBLIC MORALITY. Chicago, University of Chicago Press, 1969.
4. Coates, Joseph: WIT AND HUMOR: A NEGLECTED AID IN CROWD AND MOB CONTROL. Institute for Defense Analysis. June, 1970.
5. Cressey, Donald & Ward, David: DELINQUENCY, CRIME & SOCIAL PROCESS. New York, Harper, 1969.
6. Davidson, Henry: FORENSIC PSYCHIATRY. New York, Ronald, 1952.
7. Dieckmann, Edward & Mahendy, William: PRACTICAL HOMICIDE INVESTIGATION. Springfield, Thomas, 1961.
8. Halleck, Seymour: PSYCHIATRY & THE DILEMMAS OF CRIME. New York, Harper, 1967.
9. Hoffer, A. & Osmond, H.: THE HALLUCINOGENS. New York, Academic Press, 1967.
10. Hollister, Leo: CHEMICAL PSYCHOSES. Springfield, Thomas, 1968.
11. Karpman, Benjamin: THE SEXUAL OFFENDER AND HIS OFFENSES. New York, Julian, 1954.
12. Kling, S.: SEXUAL BEHAVIOR AND THE LAW. New York, Geis, 1965.
13. McDonald, John M.: THE MURDERER AND HIS VICTIM. Springfield, Thomas, 1961.
14. Menninger, Karl: THE CRIME OF PUNISHMENT. New York, Viking, 1966.

15. Roche, Philip: THE CRIMINAL MIND. New York, Farrar, Straus, 1958.
16. Thorwald, Jurgen: CRIME AND SCIENCE. New York, Harcourt, 1966.
17. Wolfgang, Marvin E. & Ferracuti, Franco: SUBCULTURE OF VIOLENCE. Tavistock Publications, 1967.

Chapter 9

THE RESEARCH ROLE

IN 1931, a national commission report indicated that the literature shows that, "Police work is rapidly becoming a scientific procedure in which men are given professional education, are trained to use the latest resources of modern science and to employ trained intelligence as a substitute for that of mere force which is too often regarded as chief reliance of the policeman" (21). More recently another national commission said, "The scientific and technological revolution that has so radically changed most of the American society during the past few decades has had surprisingly little impact upon the criminal justice system" (20). In emphasizing and restating this last notion a well-known police chief suggested that "Research should be a program of discovery and design and not merely patching the dike ... This nation's knowledge explosion has so far left police work untouched" (17).

The seeming contradiction between the two national commissions can perhaps best be understood in terms of the directions and emphases that research is taking within police departments rather than on the question of what research is being done and how much. I think there is no doubt that for may years leading police departments have been utilizing technological research findings and innovations. Electronic broadcasting and monitoring, computer printouts, modern crime laboratory techniques and automated data information systems have been incorporated fairly rapidly when it becomes apparent that their application will improve police functioning. Today, the emphaisis in police departments, as with most other industrial organizations, is still on the mechanical-technical approach to problem solving. Less thought and consideration seems to be given to the human side, although it is people who are involved in the social systems with which we are concerned. As Singer notes, "In spite of all of the talk about crime and violence, the average policeman spends most of his time dealing with human problems and public service. The better trained, more sensitive professional will be called on more frequently as we begin to recognize his role as a social scientist as well as law enforcement officer" (23).

Another approach which needs increased inputs in law enforcement as well as in other helping professions is that of primary prevention. The usual practice seems to be closing the barn door after the horse is gone rather than taking more economical preventive steps. As Wickersham in 1931 put it, "Crime prevention in all its ramifications is the frontier of criminology" (21). Police administrators today are more aware of the importance of psychological factors in the many areas of police work, and forward-looking departments are beginning to utilize behavioral science expertise more in this connection (19).

LIAISON WITH OTHER PROFESSIONALS

Nationally, a strategy for reducing crime was proposed by the President's Commission on Law Enforcement and the Administration of Justice under Article I of the Omnibus Crime Control and Safe Streets Act. The funding of this legislation supports research including new equipment, crime control techniques and the establishment of the National Research Institute which was founded to conduct research and development programs to reduce crime and improve the administration of justice. The Institute's goal is to apply the research data and techniques garnered from the social and physical sciences, systems analysis, operations research, psychology and management to motivate cooperation between research institutions and local law enforcement agencies (1).

Representative of the recent research programs funded nationally by LEAA are: an award of $49,885 to the Miami Police Department to study the effects of fatigue, stress and personality on police performance; a $49,815 grant to the Bureau of Social Science Research to study the uses of public opinion data in criminal justice planning; a $31,045 grant to the Washington, D. C. Department of Corrections to test the effectiveness of using rehabilitated ex-offenders as parole officers; and $11,871 to the Burk Foundation for Education at San Francisco State College to analyze relationships among crime control agencies in San Mateo (4).

Notable research around the country in the human relations area is reflected in the following examples: the work of Steinberg at the Los Angeles Police Academy utilizing small group discussions (15); a study of police selection in the Chicago Police department by Baehr and associates (2); the work of Bard in the New York Police Department in training a special policeman unit to handle family disputes (3); the Houston "sensitivity" group confrontation experiment (22); a pilot project by Glaser and associates on the Redondo Beach, Calif. Police Department to sensitize policemen in handling interpersonal conflict situations (9).

Overall, it appears there has been a slow shift in police work from purely technological research with emphasis on equipment needs to the inclusion of human relations and psychological variables in the design and implementation of research projects. Ideally, a balance should be maintained between instrumentation technology and human technology with the implicit understanding that they are in reality interacting and not exclusive.

ASSESSING IN-HOUSE RESEARCH NEEDS

One of the important assignments of the police psychologist is the development and implementation of applied research in many significant areas of police functioning. Among the difficulties of doing research within a police department is that of assessing in-house research needs. There is normally a plethora of possible research areas and it must be decided which are the most critical. This requires discussion and clarification with line personnel and administrators as well as considering only the behavioral scientist's options. It will also lead to the subsequent question of whether to contract out the research project to a consulting firm or to accomplish it in-house. The decision will hinge partly on the available resources within the police department in terms of manpower, space, expertise, confidentiality and the probability of contamination by research bias (11).

DEVELOPING AND IMPLEMENTING RESEARCH

Once the critical in-house research areas are defined, the next step is developing an adequate model. In the past, conflict frequently developed over the issue of statistical precision versus meaningful content. However, in the police field the questions to be researched are usually meaningful in terms of content. The emphasis then shifts to the kind of evaluation that should be done and what measures should be used to accomplish it. Pragmatically, this is important if the research findings are to be judged objectively and have wide applicability.

The Task Force Report on Police noted that, "Developing adequate research in a police department will require some specialization. It has, in recent years, become common for a police agency to establish a planning and research unit and to assign a number of police personnel to such a unit. But their function, until now, has focused almost exclusively upon the analysis and improvement of internal managerial and operating procedures, such as the deployment of manpower, evaluation of equipment and the streamlining of clerical procedures. In the creation of a research staff an effort should be made to utilize the rich and untapped knowledge of experienced police officers and also the knowledge and techniques of behavioral scientists . . ." (25).

In the Los Angeles Police Department, some of the research planned or underway includes: the Basic Car Plan which assigns nine radio car policemen responsibility for a specific geographic area and has them hold regular monthly meetings with citizens in their territory in order to improve channels of communication and mutual trust; a survey of the incidence of family disputes to determine the need for additional specialized training in this area; developing a small group discussion approach in addition to the current driver training program to provide inputs on the psychological side in reducing preventable traffic accidents and damage to city property; a grant proposal to examine the current selection and psychological predictors of job success; conducting a survey and developing a training proposal to better equip policemen to handle high-speed pursuits and shootings by conditioning them through simulation and cognitive approaches; assigning credentialed policemen to secondary schools to teach law enforcement, political and social science as a way of reducing friction and misunderstanding between students and policemen.

The police psychologist, like others working in various clinics, agencies and institutions, will need to develop skill in grantsmanship and applied research design including budgeting, program evaluation and statistical sophistication. This also requires some knowledge of where the research emphases and the funding are in those federal and local agencies concerned with law enforcement and police functions. It includes keeping in touch with other organizations that are also interested and involved in such research. This typically involves police departments, the International Association of Chiefs of Police, the Peace Officers Standard and Training Commission and the State and Local Universities.

ANATOMY OF A RESEARCH PROJECT

An interesting and innovative project was begun in the Los Angeles Police Department in 1970 after considerable planning and discussion. In collaboration with Dr. Robert Sokol of the Los Angeles County Department of Mental Health, we developed a pilot project to test the feasibility of training sergeants who are first-line field supervisors in the early warning recognition of emotional disturbances in their men and in brief crisis intervention techniques. Based on the concept of primary prevention, this program was designed to minimize the probability of the development of major crises and to broaden the base of awareness, understanding and sensitivity of supervisors to the emotional problems of policemen. An additional feature of this program was the assignment of experienced mental health consultants to the two experimental geographic divisions to aid the division commander and his staff in maximizing human relations effectiveness both in the department and in community relations areas. A third geographic division was used as a control. Unfortunately, major transfers from the experimental and control divisions, as well as substitution of consultants and commanders of those divisions, made it impossible to get objective before and after measures.

During twelve hours of instruction the sergeants received several blocks of information on emotional development: stress and personality; early warning signs of emotional upset; crisis intervention techniques; referral criteria; counseling limits; referral resources and consultation opportunities. This training did not attempt to make junior psychiatrists out of the sergeants but was instead designed to help them be better supervisors by increasing their responsiveness to their men as people rather than as units to be deployed.

The evaluation portion of this pilot projected utilized before and after measures of attitude and supervisory ability as well as rating scales during and at the end of different phases. It was felt that an important part of the consultation protion would be ongoing meetings with the division commander, the mental health consultants, the department psychologist and the senior psychiatric consultant in order to coordinate the various activities at the division level, and to maintain the philosophy and integrity of the program (24). The feedback from the pilot project, which was obtained by rating scales and subjective evaluations, indicated that the sergeants, the commanders, the psychiatric consultants and the program coordinators were largely positive, and most sergeants stated that they would like more training in the mental health area. Another subjective index was the increase in referrals from the two participating experimental divisions of men identified as having problems and in need of professional level assistance. Most of these referrals were by first-level supervisors. At the end of the year, the program was felt to be positive enough to write a grant proposal for federal funds to expand it to all of the geographic divisions within the police department (see Appendix III).

SOME PROBLEMS IN THE RESEARCH AREA

One of the difficulties encountered in the area of in-house research is the development of a liaison with other professionals in order to enhance behavioral science capabilities. In this connection we have established a Behavioral Science Resource Committee consisting of psychologists and psychiatrists from the community who are donating their time and expertise in support of psychological programs within the Department. This group meets on a monthly basis to discuss current developments. Another problem involves the personalities of the researchers and their naivete about police operations and functions. Obviously this can lead to communication difficulties and lack of understanding regarding the police work about which they are trying to be helpful. We have found it necessity, almost routinely, to have research people and consultants undergo an orientation and familiarization training period whereby they ride in police cars and learn about police work before they attempt a contribution from their own professional perspective. Another important question related to in-house research is that of manpower needs and cost effectiveness. Typically, large police departments are undermanned and have recruiting problems. Therefore, it becomes a crucial issue when the assignment of manpower to nonpolice functions considered peripheral has to be justified both administratively and politically. Additionally, there is the necessity of having adequately trained personnel to perform research functions. "Perhaps the most critical problem is the limited number of people with the talent and perseverance to direct and work within such organizations. Intellectual capacity must be combined with a relatively rare ability to reevaluate continually, not only the assumptions and programs of existing agencies, but one's own biases and commitments as well" (7).

Another problem which is common to most organizations is that of communication within a multilevel system and the difficult of maintaining a two-way network in order to avoid overlap and redundancy. The President's Commission mentions the additional problems of resistance to innovations, suspiciousness of outsiders, and fear of criticism (20). However, I don't think that these reactions are peculiar to police organizations, but are also found in institutions of medicine, education, law, psychology and others.

BIBLIOGRAPHY

1. A UNITED STRATEGY FOR CRIME CONTROL. L.E.A.A., Department of Justice, 1968, pp. 14-15.
2. Baehr, M. et al.: PSYCHOLOGICAL ASSESSMENT OF PATROLMAN

QUALIFICATIONS IN RELATION TO FIELD PERFORMANCE. L.E.A.A., Department of Justice, November 1968.
3. Bard, M. and Berkowitz, B.: Training police as specialists in family crisis intervention: a community psychology action program. COMMUNITY MENTAL HEALTH JOURNAL, 3:4, pp. 315-317, winter 1967.
4. BEHAVIORAL SCIENCE NEWSLETTER. American Institutes for Research, Pittsburgh, May 22, 1970 p. 3.
5. Blumstein, A.: A NATIONAL PROGRAM OF RESEARCH, DEVELOPMENT AND EVALUATION ON LAW ENFORCEMENT AND CRIMINAL JUSTICE. Institute for Defense Analysis, November 1968.
6. Buckley, W. (Ed.): MODERN SYSTEMS RESEARCH FOR THE BEHAVIORAL SCIENTIST. Chicago, Aldine, 1968.
7. Doig, J. W.: The police in a democratic society: police problems, proposals and strategies for change. PUBLIC ADMINISTRATION REVIEW, p. 401, September-October 1968.
8. Fairweather, G. W.: METHODS FOR EXPERIMENTAL SOCIAL INNOVATION. New York, Wiley, 1968.
9. Glaser, E. M.: A PROGRAM TO TRAIN POLICE OFFICERS TO INTERVENE IN FAMILY DISTURBANCES. Final Report for L.E.A.A. Human Inter-Action Research Institute, Los Angeles, April 1970.
10. Keniston, K.: Quoted in CONFRONTATION, Newsletter, Lemberg Center for the Study of Violence. Brandeis University, April 1970.
11. Kerlinger, F.: FOUNDATIONS OF BEHAVIORAL RESEARCH. New York, Holt, Rinehart and Winston, 1967.
12. KNOWLEDGE INTO ACTION: IMPROVING THE NATION'S USE OF THE SOCIAL SCIENCES. National Science Foundation, 1969.
13. Levy, R. and Cook, R.: INVESTIGATION OF A METHOD FOR IDENTIFICATION OF THE HIGH-RISK POLICE APPLICANT. Mimeo, 1970.
14. Marris, P. and Rein, M.: DILEMMAS OF SOCIAL REFORM. New York, Atherton, 1969.
15. Newman, L. E. and Steinberg, J. L.: Consultation with police on human relations training. AMERICAN JOURNAL OF PSYCHIATRY, 126:10, pp. 65-73, April 1970.
16. Oppenheim, A. N.: QUESTIONNAIRE DESIGN AND ATTITUDE MEASUREMENT. New York, Basic Books, 1966.
17. Reddin, T.: Police weapons for the space age. THE POLICE CHIEF, pp. 10-17, November 1966.
18. Reiser, M.: The police department psycholgist. POLICE, pp. 24-25, January-February 1970.
19. Reiser, M.: The police psychologist as consultant. POLICE, pp. 58-60 January-February 1971.
20. REPORT OF THE NATIONAL ADVISORY COMMISSION ON CIVIL DISORDERS. New York, Bantam, 1968.
21. REPORT ON POLICE. National Commission on Law Observance and

Enforcement (Wickersham), United States Government Printing Office, 1931.
22. Sikes, M. P. and Cleveland, S. E.: Human relations training for police and community. AMERICAN PSYCHOLOGIST, 24:8 pp. 766-769, August 1969.
23. Singer, H. A.: The cop as social scientist. THE POLICE CHIEF, pp. 52-58, April 1970.
24. Sokol, R. and Reiser, M.: A PRIMARY PREVENTION PROPOSAL UTILIZING EARLY WARNING TRAINING AND DIVISION MENTAL HEALTH CONSULTANTS. Los Angeles Police Department, October 1969.
25. TASK FORCE REPORT: THE POLICE. The President's Commission on Law Enforcement and Administration of Justice, 1967.
26. THE CHALLENGE OF CRIME IN A FREE SOCIETY. The President's Commission on Law Enforcement and Administration of Justice, 1967.
27. TO ESTABLISH JUSTICE, TO INSURE DOMESTIC TRANQUILITY. Final Report of the National Commission on the Causes and Prevention of Violence, December 1969.

Chapter 10

SOME PROBLEMS AND DILEMMAS ORGANIZATIONAL AND PERSONAL

CONFIDENTIALITY

BECAUSE much of the personal-problem, marital and family counseling that the psychologist does is personal and involves a privileged counselor-client relationship, some men feel suspicious and distrustful and hesitate to use a helping resource within the department. Although there are potential situations where the limits of confidentiality can be unclear and controversial, in practice I have found that this is not a widespread problem. In general, when the problems are of a personal nature, whether marital, job related or family, if there are no criminal activities involved and the person is in control, rational, and capable of self-care, there is no problem about maintaining the confidentiality of the relationship. However, if the individual is psychotic, destructively acting-out, engaged in serious criminal activity, suicidal or homicidal, then the need for confidentiality is overridden by the greater need to protect the individual and the community. This also applies to the professional in private practice in the community as outlined in the ethical principles of psychiatrists, psychologists and social workers. In situations where a man has come in for confidential counseling and later gets involved in an offense which results in an investigation by Internal Affairs, the investigators are usually very cooperative and understanding when the limits of confidentiality are spelled out. In some instances they have secured written release forms from the individual so that information can be communicated more easily. In a large portion of these situations, the information is more likely to be helpful than detrimental to the individual under investigation. For example, it may be used to bolster his defense at a Board of Rights hearing. By meeting with each recruit and sergeants' class, and by making this distinction clear, over a period of time there is a greater trust and willingness to come in voluntarily to discuss problems of a personal nature without fear of jeopardizing one's promotion, job status or manliness.

SERVICE VERSUS STAFF CONFLICTS

In providing confidential counseling services to policemen and families it is important to maintain the distinction between the service and staff function. At times the administration may ask the psychologist to function in his staff role in a way which may compromise him with an individual or group of policemen within the organization. In such a situation the psychologist should explain that this would place him in a dilemma by putting a negative coloration on his role which would easily sabatoge the long-range goals he is trying to achieve. Typically, administrators with whom I have worked have been quick to see the point.

Another problem that comes up at times is the amount of time the psychologist invests in direct services as opposed to his time in consultant functions. Normally, a clinical psychologist spends about one third of his time doing therapy with the balance of his time divided among administrative detail, professional upgrading, research, training, keeping up with the literature, writing for publications and attending conferences. One of the difficulties in a one-man psychological services operation is a tendency for increased requests for counseling over time and for a similar increase in consultation projects. These requests include assistance with research projects, teaching recruits, sergeants and above, training, programming, writing handbooks and reports, sitting on review boards and committees and others. There is a need to maintain a balance between service and staff functions so that many of the pressing issues get handled promptly without anyone feeling rejected or that service is inadequate in a special area. This is an extremely difficult arrangement considering that at least a half dozen staff people would be necessary to perform all of the functions that one man is attempting to do.

MAINTAINING PROFESSIONAL OBJECTIVITY AND IDENTITY

One of the deeper problems affecting the psychologist in a large task-oriented organization is that of maintaining his individuality and professional autonomy while being aware of the constant shaping influences on him by his organization and his assigned role. Most institutions exert pressures to conform and to accept the organizational standards, attitudes and values, both positive and negative. There is also the unconscious need to identify with the organization in order to belong and to conform to peer group norms. I think an optimal amount of identification is necessary and unavoidable. However, the psychologist should be aware that this is taking place so that he can retain some control over decision-making and over the extent of his uncritical acceptance of institutionalized values. These values are constantly changing even if ever so slowly, sometimes to the point of extinction.

In this regard I have found it helpful to maintain contact with other behavioral professionals who are usually quite adept at challenging different viewpoints and providing new inputs and perspectives. This can give much food for though and require a continual reassessment of one's attitudes and values in order to maintain a comfortable, workable balance.

THE "HEADSHRINKER" VERSUS THE "COP"

Just as there is some antipathy between so-called liberals and conservatives, there tends to be some suspiciousness, resistance and negative feeling between mental health professionals and men in police work. I think this is partly because the mental health professionals are judged to be overly permissive and are perhaps to some degree more forgiving, understanding and less judgmental. However, men in police work tend to be more practical, more pessimistic and yet more realistic. In part, this is because they are not permitted the luxury of theorizing, second-guessing or having a large amount of time to make a decision. The very nature of the police function requires adherence to rules, the framework of written law which helps shape the man in police work in the direction of pragmatism and conservatism. This results in a further effort to maintain a status quo which is actually in flux. However, I have the impression that this situation is being changed gradually. The young men entering police work tend to have more formal education in the social sciences and humanities and as they become more professionalized, taking on more of the social-helping functions, they will move closer in identity and in practice to the behavioral scientist. Current fads to the contrary, I think that most mental health professionals see the setting of realistic limits as necessary in child development to achieve mental health and adequate personality and character structure. I think the net result over time will be the diminishing of the perceived distance between the psychologist and the policeman.

THE UNCONSULTANT

Because managers in an organization tend to view the scientist consultant with some apprehension and fear, perhaps unconsciously suspecting magical powers, mind reading or brainwashing ability, the psychologist working in a police department must counter this tendency by adaptability and by his human as well as scientific qualities. He needs to have a positive view of people and not stereotype or label them in a pejorative way, especially those coming to him for assistance with problems. Hodges (2) points out that several negative attitudes in the consultant guarantee ruining the consultation process. The first attitude is that the consultant's knowledge is sacred and he can communicate it only to a chosen few. This effectively helps maintain or even increase the distance which tends to be present between the consultant and the management in the organization. The second negative attitude is the consultant's inordinate need for respect, status and adoration which he tries to satisfy in his relationships with the people with whom he deals. In this regard he attempts to put himself on a pedestal which then changes the nature of the consultation to parent-child instead of equal adults discussing a problem. The third attitude is that the image of "expert" be maintained at all costs, communicating that the consultee is inferior and should acknowledge it. Of course, no consultant has all the answers and should readily admit to that fact rather than attempt to present an aura of omniscience to the consultee. In my experience, there are few pat formulas for success as a consultant. Actually what a consultant does is a function of the role expectations of the organization, plus what expertise the consultant brings to the situation including his personal attributes.

BIBLIOGRAPHY

1. Drucker, Peter: MANAGING FOR RESULTS. New York, Harper, 1966
2. Hodges, Allen: How not to be a consultant. MENTAL HYGIENE, 54:1 pp. 147-148, January, 1970.

Chapter 11

PROFESSIONAL GROWTH

IN spite of the fact that I had over thirteen years of experience in various aspects of clinical, educational and community psychology before coming to work for the Los Angeles Police Department, I found that in many ways I was starting at the beginning. I had to broaden my capabilities and change perspectives in dealing with previously unencountered problems and situations. One of the first things I found myself doing was reading a tremendous amount of literature on police subjects, delinquency and the criminal justice system. I also began assembling a bibliography of what I considered writings having a direct bearing on my job. This meant filling in an area where my background was sketchy and staying with it because of the increasing amount of material continually published in psychological and other areas of police systems and work. In addition to keeping abreast of new developments and theories, it is vitally necessary for the psychologist to continue his growth in the practical aspects of police work and the attendant problems. It is helpful to go out on patrol once a month in a different division of the city to stay in touch with the problems of the men in patrol so that they are not just case histories or clinical oddities.

As the psychologist becomes accepted in the organization and the requests for his service increase, he can plan and recommend needed expansion of psychological services with security and justification. He will need to assess and to document the need very carefully in terms of direct services, training, consultation and research and then convince the administration that additional professional staff is necessary to adequately perform increased old functions and the new ones which continually proliferate. With additional assistance, particularly in the counseling area, the department psychologist can get more involved in management development programs, systems approaches and in top-level management consultation. The need is great and the payoff potentially significant.

Chapter 12

THE FUTURE

SOME DESIRABLE DIRECTIONS AND DEVELOPMENTS

I THINK the increasing emphasis on behavioral science inputs in police departments will help to better counterbalance the technological-mechanistic approaches that have been more usual. I also see more attention focused on the concept of primary prevention and on developing prevention approaches with impact. There will aslo be the realization and acceptance of the reality of interacting social systems in confronting causal factors rather than the old futile approach of piecemeal plugging of the dike after leaks have already sprung. Police departments will not only increasingly utilize psychological and other behavioral science professionals in various areas of police work as a routine matter, but will also train more policemen at undergraduate and graduate levels in the behavioral science specialties.

Technological leaps will probably continue and it will require continued focus and emphasis on the human variables to close the gap rather than widen it. At the present time, our knowledge and ability to function effectively in areas of human relations is far behind our technological capabilities. It is primarily up to the behavioral sciences to lessen the distance between hardware and human values and thus earn a more equitable role.

"Every past attempt at prophesy has turned out to be grieviously incorrect. Extrapolations from the past, while sometimes useful, are usually fundamentally wrong in the long run, expecially when they attempt to predict the quality of human life, the nature of political and social organization, international relations, or the shape of future cultures . . . Technology is not an inevitable master of man and history, but merely provides the possiblity of applying scientific knowledge to specific problems" (1).

BIBLIOGRAPHY

1. Keniston, Kenneth: Quoted in CONFRONTATION. Newsletter, Lemberg Center for the Study of Violence, Brandeis University, April 1970.

Appendix I

SOME TYPICAL PROJECTS AND REQUESTS OF DEPARTMENT PSYCHOLOGISTS

1. Survey involvement of policemen in mentally ill and suicidal cases in Los Angeles Police Department.
2. Consult on design of a new driver training program with emphasis on psychological and emotional factors.
3. Help design a prototype training program on shooting and decision-making under stress.
4. Infer a psychological protrait of suspect under surveillance by intelligence officers and predict likelihood of homicidal behavior.
5. Assist in designing a Department-wide career guidance program.
6. Consult with community relations specialists on making a valid survey of community feelings and attitudes toward the Department.
7. Aid in designing a research project to evaluate the methods and cost effectiveness of recruitment.
8. Consult with Homicide Division detectives on bizarre aspects of multiple murders.
9. Participate in a joint task force to develop a liaison research group with university and Department cooperation.
10. Conduct a pilot study on optimal I.Q. needs of Los Angeles policemen and criteria of success on the job.
11. Assist division detectives in aiding a witness to a felony accurately recall the numbers on suspect's license plate.
12. Design, implement and coordinate a pilot project to train sergeants in mental health techniques.
13. Help evaluate a pilot research project utilizing trained policemen as discussion group leaders in public secondary schools.
14. Teach basic counseling principles to new sergeants.

15. Write a human relations handbook for policemen on the street.
16. Testify as an expert witness on pornography prosecutions.
17. Consult with policemen-teachers on their counseling role in the public school.
18. Survey the divorce experience in the Department to get actual facts to replace rumors.
19. Teach unit on social development to juvenile investigators.

Appendix II

HUMAN RELATIONS HANDBOOK FOR POLICE OFFICERS
(Sample Format)

With the Collaboration of
J. Leonard Steinberg, Ed.D.

PREFACE

The Los Angeles Police Department is acknowledged as one of the finest in the world. It is important that we continually improve our performance in maintaining that regard.

This handbook is intended to aid officers of this Department by alerting them to those critical areas of police-citizen contact with most often engender complaints. These complaints typically spring from routine transactions which have been mishandled, creating a negative experience for officer and citizen alike.

By focusing on identified problems, we can use a problem-solving approach to minimize the possiblity of conflict and negative reactions while maximizing efficiency and positive personal contacts.

Many of the complaints from both citizens and policemen center around problems in communication and attitude. Of course, this is a two-way street, with citizens as well as police officers having responsibility for courtesy, self-control and consideration of the other person. We all need to recognize the complex nature of social problems in a changing society and to work cooperatively to achieve mutual respect and a law-abiding community.

CONTENTS

Preface
  I. THE POLICEMAN'S ROLE IN TODAY'S COMMUNITY
     Law Enforcement
     Crime Prevention
     Service Functions
     Ethnic Composition of Los Angeles
 II. WHAT ARE POLICEMEN REALLY LIKE?
     Stress Occupations and Need for Balance in Personal and Professional Life
     Importance of Self-Image on Security
     Difference Between Thoughts and Actions
     Intelligence, Emotional Stability and Needs – Actions, Recognition, Responsibility
     The Need for a Sense of Humor
III. PITFALL – PROBLEMS OF ATTITUDE
     Cynical Attitude – Everyone an Idiot
     Intolerance, Prejudice and Ethnocentrism
     Stereotyping Minorities – Ethnic, Tenagers, Women, Long Hair, Old Cars
     Superior Attitude (Badge Heavy) – Insecurity
     Attitudes Shape Behavior and Affect Image
 IV. PITFALL – PROBLEMS OF COMMUNICATION
     Words Are Tools of Trade
     Courtesy, How It Is Said – Tone and Manner
     Profanity, Name-Calling, Excessive Familiarity
     Nonverbal-Finger Stabbing, Pushing, Turning Away
     The Power of Listening
     Explaining Actions – Prevent Anger and Resentment
     Overseriousness an Occupational Hazard
  V. PITFALL – PROBLEMS OF ANGER AND PROVOCATION
     Hostility Is Contagious – by Citizen, Suspect or Officer
     Policeman as Authority Symbol
     Being Manipulated into "Proving" Yourself
     A Basic Question – "Whose Problem Is It?"
 VI. WHAT IS A PROFESSIONAL POLICEMAN?
     Objective Rather Than Personal Reactions
     Impartial – Firm but Fair
     Constructive Use of Discretion
     Maintain Ethical Standards – with Citizens and Colleagues

I. THE POLICEMAN'S ROLE IN TODAY'S COMMUNITY

In society's day-to-day efforts to protect its citizens from the suffering, fear and property loss produced by crime and the threat of crime, the policeman occupies the front line. It is he who directly confronts criminal situations, and it is to him that the public looks for personal safety. The freedom of Americans to walk their streets and be secure in their homes — in fact to do what they want when they want — depends to a great extent on their policeman.

The President's Commission on Law Enforcement

Today, more than ever before, the police profession is unique in its demands. A policeman in today's society must be a highly trained professional, competent to adequately fill the many roles that complex police work involves. He must routinely function as partly lawyer, psychologist, teacher, social worker, criminologist and public relations expert. But a policeman is more than just a professional. He is also a public official with considerable power and responsibility. He is sworn to protect and to serve the citizens of the community without fear or favoritism. One man's attitude or one street encounter can represent the entire Department in the community. Bad community feeling not only causes tension and divisiveness between the public and the police, but it tends to stimulate crime, which in turn increases police problems.

The very nature of the patrolman's job forces him into the areas where various elements of society clash. This creates a need for understanding on the part of police officers and on the part of the community members that they are attempting to serve. If understanding is lacking, then decision-making, judgment, and general performance in the field will be less effective. In this regard, policemen must be willing to adapt to rapid changes in social behavior patterns, even if they seem different or annoying. The main question is, has there been a violation of the law?

Although law enforcement is an important priority function, a large part of the time, police work is a public service or helping occupation requiring high-level interpersonal skills. Former Chief William H. Parker has stated that, "Public service is one of the noblest professions." In order to function effectively in this crucial area of police-citizen contact, the professional policeman must be able to communicate clearly and to maintain positive attitudes about the citizens he serves.

Another important and often overlooked function of the police officer is crime prevention. Heading off crime is much more economical in terms of time, effort and money than trying to catch and rehabilitate criminals. In addition to suppressing crime by their visibility in a community, policemen can achieve long-range preventive effects by helping to educate the general public about police problems and by developing good relations with children and juveniles. In providing positive models with which children may identify, policemen may not only prevent future crime, but also influence character development in a positive direction. These are also some of the main goals of the Basic Car Plan which assigns selected officers these responsibilities for their district.

It is anticipated that by the middle 1970's more than half of the people living in Los Angeles will be members of minority groups. Thus, increasingly, the citizens that the Los Angeles Police Department is serving are people from the Mexican-American, Negro, Oriental, and Puerto Rican communities. Although police officers should not be expected to solve the accumulated problems of generations of social inequity, the primary responsibility for attempting improvement in relationships between police and members of minority communities must begin with the organized professionals — the police. As Chief Parker noted, "inconguities in this relation must be adjusted and the responsibility rests primarily with the police. It is therefore our task to adjust our procedures and techniques in line with public receptivity without sacrificing efficiency and without departing from the objectives and purposes of the police service. It is a difficult adjustment but the challenge cannot be ignored."

II. WHAT ARE POLICEMEN REALLY LIKE?

> The complexities inherent in the policing function dictate that officers possess a high degree of intelligence, education, tact, sound judgement, physical courage, emotional stability, impartiality and honesty...
>
> *The President's Commission on Law Enforcement*

There is no such thing as a police personality. Rather, there is a variety of individual personalities who choose a career in the police profession. Studies on men coming into police work indicate that they are above average in intelligence, are more emotionally stable than the average population and are usually motivated by the needs for action, recognition and responsibility. Men in police work tend to be conscientious, energetic and ambitious and are interested in upgrading themselves by achieving higher educational and occupational status. In addition, they desire to make the community a better place in which to live.

Men in police work are also human beings and subject to the same kinds of feelings and tensions as other people. Along with several other professions including psychiatry, air traffic control work and space engineering, police work is considered a stress occupation. The multiple pressures of the job create an added burden on the man which may affect his physical emotional and personal well-being. In order to adapt to the increased stresses in police work, it is important for officers to have a stable home life. In addition, outside interests in sports and hobbies, or avocations are desirable to counterbalance the tensions and demands of the profession. Counseling assistance is available in the Department for those who have stress-related problems.

To feel self-confident and to function effectively, the man in police work needs a good measure of inner security. To feel secure, he must have a positive self-image. That is, he has to like himself as a person — think he is worthwhile and on a par with other people in the world. Without this positive sense of self the man in police work is likely to be overly anxious, insecure and consequently less able to efficiently handle a wide range of problems and people.

Policemen should be aware that there is a big difference between what a person thinks and what he does. Everyone is entitled to his thoughts no matter how silly or bizarre. This includes policemen as well as other citizens. Problems arise when thoughts are equated with actions or are acted upon. When this happens, others' rights are likely to be affected. Thinking something is not a crime, but putting the thought into action may well be. Our concern is not what a man thinks but what he does.

A good sense of humor is an asset to the man in police work. The ability to see humor in some situations can help ease tension, lessen the burden and keep many incidents interesting which might otherwise have become difficult and frustrating. The ability to laugh at oneself is one indicator of a well-developed sense of humor.

III. PITFALL – PROBLEMS OF ATTITUDE

> With a ratio of only one policeman for 500 other people, the only way we can survive and be successful is to enlist and obtain the support of the citizenry at large in helping us protect and serve them.
>
> *Chief Edward M. Davis*

In police work, as in other professions, a certain amount of skepticism is health and can even save your life. It means alertness and not taking things for granted, even apparently routine situation.

Problem: A Cynical Attitude

A cynical attitude means a negative view of life — everybody is an idiot and nothing is any good. The extreme cynical attitude is usually accompanied by depression or anger, or both. A depressed or angry man cannot function as efficiently as a calm, optimistic one. In addition, this attitude is certain to be communicated to other people and will likely influence routine matters on the street in a negative way. Policemen are repeatedly exposed to a relatively small group of people which includes criminals, suspects, people with problems of living and citizens who do not like policemen or police work. This increases the tendency to develop tunnel vision and generalize from a relatively small sample to the whole community.

Although its origin is undertandable, the cynical attitude is nonproductive and undesirable in the professional police officer.

Problem: Intolerance, Prejudice and Ethnocentrism

A policeman, like any other citizen is entitled to his private biases and personal feelings. However, when thes attitudes determine the manner in which he approaches and deals with people on the job, then his effectiveness as a Los Angeles policeman is diminished.

Narrow-mindedness and prejudice are partly related to a lack of information and education as well as a need to overvalue what is familiar and thus "true." What is familiar tends to be comforting and what is unfamiliar tends to produce anxiety and thus seems a threat.

Ethnocentrism is an attitude of superiority in regard to ethnic groups that are different. The ethnocentric is incapable of evaluating other cultures logically and unemotionally. He, inappropriately, tries to judge other groups by the standards and practices of his own subculture. This results in looking down on other groups as inferior — a view directly contrary to the basic notion of equality among peoples in a democratic society. Intolerance and prejudgments that affect the police officer's behavior are handicaps which must be examined, acknowledged and controlled.

Problem: Stereotyping

Stereotypes are labels a person uses to lump together all members of a particular group. Stereotypes are cliches which can be applied to ethnic groups, teenagers, women, long hair, old cars or any subgroup which is looked on as different and thus inferior. Within each minority group there are individuals whose life styles, value systems and political points of view are varied, so that labeling is not only a denial of individuality, it is also inaccurate. Policemen have long experience with being stereotyped as a group and so should be sensitive to this problem in regard to other minorities.

Within the Los Angeles Police Department, men and women of all ethnic, religious and cultural backgrounds are employed on an integrated, equal basis. Remarks, actions or jokes which can be interpreted as insults, even unintentionally, should be avoided.

Problem: A Superior Attitude

Complaints frequently result when an officer approaches citizens with an officious or superior attitude. A heavy-handed, belittling badge-heavy manner actually reveals the policeman's own insecurity and the attempt to compensate for it in his behavior. The secure individual is confident, authoritative and nondefensive rather than demeaning or overly aggressive. All people are equal under the law and even individuals who commit serious violations must be treated as human beings who will likely return to society.

Very quickly, the officer on patrol learns that attitudes affect behavior. He finds that his own way of approaching a person tends to determine the kind of response. He also finds that the citizen's attitude toward him tends to produce certain inner feelings. But because he is a trained professional, the police officer knows he isn't permitted to act on his personal feelings or impulses. He is aware that if he does, his career as well as the Department's image can be damaged. Experienced policemen have learned that it is easier to talk a person into the station than to fight him in.

IV. PITFALL – PROBLEMS OF COMMUNICATION

Because police work is an occupation that deals mainly with people, words are one of the most powerful tools of the trade. But there is more to communication than just words. There are also the many subtle nonverbal messages that speak volumes.

Problem: Discourtesy

The tone of voice and manner of speaking can convey messages which reinforce or cancel out the words used. When we treat others with courtesy and consideration, we are clearly setting the level and tone for the kind of transaction we expect. Most people tend to respond to these expectations. In general, respect for other people is usually a reflection of one's self-respect.

Problem: Profanity, Name-Calling, Excessive Familiarity

Cursing at or calling people uncomplimentary names is unprofessional and has no place in police-citizen contacts. References to skin color, ethnic origin, physical appearance, sex or socioeconomic status are inappropriate. The proper method of address is Mr., Miss or Mrs. and the last name, even when the situation is a difficult one. The use of first names or becoming overly familiar with citizens can lead to misunderstandings and resentment. A good general rule is not to use first names unless you expect yours to be used. Teenagers are especially sensitive to a heavy-handed approach of the suggestion of being treated as children. Addressing juvenile groups as "men" or "ladies" and use of the teenager's last name communicates the expectation of adult behavior.

Problem: Nonverbal Communication

The words can be exact but the communication received may be exactly opposite. When dealing with people, actions have priority over words in conveying feelings and intentions. Pushing someone aside, turning your back on a person while he is talking to you or punctuating remarks with a stabbing finger all containing clear messages. They signal that communicator is angry, feels threatened, lacks respect or fears losing control of the situation.

Problem: Not Listening

In people occupations, one of the least recognized yet most effective tools professionals have is listening. By carefully listening to a person, we allow him to discharge some of his pent-up emotions, lower his tension level and reduce his anxiety. Because we are willing to share his problem, he feels less alone and depressed. Simple as it sounds, interested listening is a difficult art to master. However, the experienced officer knows its value, and uses it.

Problem: Not Explaining Actions

On partol stops are often necessary which may involve a search for weapons, a want or warrant check or merely the investigation of a suspicious situation. The policeman knows why he stops someone, but the citizen may be bewildered and defensive. Most of us like to know what is happening and why something is being done to us. A simple explanation by the officer will satisfy curiosity, reduce anger and head off a possible complaint. Telling the person why he is being stopped, why handcuffs are necessary, or why a citation is being issued points out the logical, nonpersonal nature of the behavior and changes the situation from a personal encounter to a professional contact.

An explanation is neither a sign of weakness nor a pampering of the citizen. It is merely the professional approach of smoothing the way in order to get the job done with the least amount of strain.

Problem: Overseriousness

Police work involves serious and sometimes tragic human events. Repeated exposure can lead to a tendency to shut off all feelings, to appear gruff and serious to the point of coldness. This is an occupational hazard that usually diminishes with experience and the knowledge that a smile can be more effective than a frown or harsh tone. The man who doesn't take himself too seriously is probably the more stable and better adjusted individual since the ability to laugh at oneself occasionally is a measure of inner security.

V. PITFALL – PROBLEMS OF ANGER AND PROVOCATION

Routine contacts may generate in citizens fellings' of accusation, guilt, anger or resentment. This can happen without any provocation on the part of the officer. A person's hostility tends to be contagious – it stimulates defensiveness, counterhostility and raises barriers to communication. The well-trained policeman is aware of this process and is able to control his personal reactions since he knows the anger isn't directed at him personally but at him as an authority figure.

Problem: Policeman as Authority Symbol

Some individuals react negatively toward policemen in an almost automatic way. The man in uniform isn't seen as an individual but as a symbol. Badge, gun and uniform trigger guilt feelings and anger in people who have not resolved their own conflicts with authority. These individuals may actually be fighting against their problems by exaggerated reactions to authority. In order to feel more comfortable, they need to use an external authority symbol as a scapegoat. Policemen, as well as other minority groups, fill this need. In this sense, policemen serve above and beyond the call of duty without due recognition or thanks.

Problem: Being Manipulated
Into Proving Yourself

To insecure suspects, not only the uniform but also the youthful appearance or small stature of an officer can seem a challenge. The person who needs to challenge a youthful policeman will try to bait or manipulate him so that he can "prove himself a bigger man." If the officer understands the reason for this behavior, he may help defuse the situation by merely acknowledging that, "I know you're a man; you don't have to prove it." This can cut right through to the suspect's basic conflict and help to calm his anxiety over whether he is a real man.

Because the professional policeman knows his own self worth and is secure in his role, he doesn't need to demonstrate his masculinity or toughness by allowing himself to be manipulated into a fight. On the other hand, he doesn't tolerate physical abuse, and takes prompt action to contain an assaultive suspect.

Problem: Whose Problem Is It?

When handling provacative individuals, the officer must ask himself the basic question, "Whose problem is it?" Invariably, the answer will be that it is the suspect's problem. The officer then gains little by getting personally involved and making it his problem also. By recognizing the source of the problem, the policeman is able to control the situation, keep the contact and impersonal one and avoid a degrading altercation.

VI. WHAT IS A PROFESSIONAL POLICEMAN?

The mark of the professional police officer is his objectivity and the ability to maintain his coolheadedness in a variety of tense, provocative situations. He is able to step back from the emotion-charged scene and keep his long-range perspective. He keeps his professional, rather than his personal, needs primary.

The well-trained officer is fair and impartial, but also firm in his approach. His professional manner is maintained even when serious and personally distasteful crimes have been committed. In these instances, he does not see himself as a punisher because he knows he is only one aspect of the larger criminal justice system. His main goal is to get his part of the job done as efficiently as possible.

The professional policeman is aware that he cannot always enforce all laws to the letter and that he therefore must often use discretion and good judgment. He values his discretionary powers as an important responsiblity and considers what will be most beneficial to the community when making his decisions.

Like other professions, the police service has a code of ethics. This code demands that the professional officer maintain ethical standards and conduct in the performance of his duties. Ethical behavior with citizens and with colleagues means placing profession and community responsibility before self in maintaining the high principles of the police profession.

Appendix III

OUTLINE OF A RESEARCH PROJECT

A PRIMARY PREVENTION PROPOSAL UTILIZING EARLY WARNING TRAINING AND DIVISION MENTAL HEALTH CONSULTANTS

(A Cooperative Effort Between the Los Angeles Police Department and the Los Angeles County Department of Mental Health)

Robert J. Sokol,, M. D.
Senior Psychiatric Consultant to Law Enforcement Agencies, LACDMH
and

Martin Reiser, Ed.D.,
Department of Psychologist, Los Angeles Police Department

I. INTRODUCTION

THIS proposal is based on the concept of primary prevention. That is, effective early intervention will minimize the probability of a major crisis developing later. "Primary prevention encompasses actions that maximize social forces in the community which tend to encourage the full development of the human being as a rational, creative and self-actualizing organism" (1).

It is estimated that in a so-called normal population, about 23 percent of the people have emotional conflicts which are severely limiting (3). It seems predictable then, that policemen who work under unusual stresses and demands would be at least as prone to encountering emotional conflicts as those in less stressful occupational groups. The complex nature of the policeman role, including instantaneous decision-making in ambiguous and life-and-death situations, requires clear preceptions, emotional stability and levelheaded judgments. Serious emotional upset could not only impair the individual policeman's level of functioning and safety, but could also negatively affect the image of the entire Department. For these reasons, it seems desirable to broaden the base of awareness, understanding and sensitivity to emotional problems in policemen by providing more channels for detection and handling of these problems in the Department.

In addition, the constructive use of experienced mental health consultants in selected geographic divisions should aid the division commander and his staff, as well as the local community, in enhancing opportunities for positive interaction and communication around mutual concerns. In brief, the consultant can help increase human relations effectiveness.

This project would also have public relations value since it is an innovation and constitutes a first among police departments nationally. In working cooperatively with the Los Angeles County Department of Mental Health, we are indicating our ability to share problems and resources with other community agencies in striving toward common goals. This is in keeping with L.A.P.D.'s position in the forefront of modern police practice.

II. BRIEF DESCRIPTION OF PROPOSAL

This project would be implemented on an experimental basis as a pilot study for one year. There are two basic features to this proposal. First is to train sergeants — close contact line supervisors — in early detection of emotional upset and to teach them brief counseling techniques. This would increase the range of problems that could be handled in the field on early contact, preventing exacerbation in some cases and allowing appropriate further referral in others. In effect, this should make the detection, counseling and referral processes more available to the man in the field and yet more economical in resolving some problems before they become major issues. A secondary gain might be better supervision by sergeants because of their increased sensitivity to the focus on their men as people rather than as units to be deployed.

This program does not attempt to make "junior psychiatrists" out of the sergeants. In fact, awareness of their limits in the counseling role will be stressed in order to minimize any tendencies toward overzealousness.

The second part of this proposal involves the assignment of a professional mental health consultant to four selected geographic divisions on a pilot basis in cooperation with the County Department of Mental Health. The consultants would perform several important functions. They would provide the necessary backup to the "case finding" sergeants in the division by providing consultation in difficult cases as to treatment needs and referral resources. In a broader and perhaps more important way, the consultant, when requested, would also assist the division commander and his staff in areas of community relations, interpersonal situations, development of needed programs in that particular division and in other diverse ways as individual division needs suggest.

III. SCOPE OF THE PROGRAM

Objectives

Inherent in this proposal is the concept of primary prevention in minimizing the incidence of major emotional crises in individuals and in larger populations. The main goals of this proposal are two fold: first, to increase the level of functioning of the line policeman by recognizing that unique factors affect his emotional needs and to provide channels to aid him in this area; second, to broaden the base of human relations expertise and capability in selected divisions by the utilization of professionally trained consultants. These objectives would be implemented by: early detection of problems and brief counseling intervention before exacerbation occurs by providing a coordinated network of mental health services throughout the Department; adding mental health consultation at the division level to provide backup, referral, interpersonal programming, and

and other relevent assistance as requested within the division. Initially, two to four divisions should participate in the pilot phase.

Selection and Training

Sergeants

Sergeants in the division selected for this project would be trained in early recognition of emotional problems and in utilization of crisis intervention techniques. It is anticipated that a preponderance of personal problems can be handled adequately at this line level. However, referral criteria and a referral network will be included in the program. Initially, only the sergeants in the pilot project divisions will be trained. Provided the program is successful and expansion feasible, eventually all supervisors would routinely receive this training as part of the sergeants' school. Ultimately, this should increase division capability for problem solving and personnel management.

Training for the sergeants would involve approximately twelve hours. The content and presentation of the material is a key factor. The initial curriculum will be developed by the Department psychologist and the psychiatric consultant and be taught by them the first few times before revision. A policeman teacher-trainee will also participate. Subsequently, other professional staff from the Department of Mental health or university would be trained to share teaching responsibilities with the policeman-teacher in a team-teaching format. Ongoing supervison would be provided by Department psychologist and psychiatric consultant.

The twelve hours of instruction would be divided into four three-hour segments. Because instruction must be interesting and dynamic to succeed, techniques such as role playing, simulations, case reports and videotape feedback would be used, as well as the usual audiovisual methods. The three-hour segments would be divided as follows: emotional development, stress and personality; early warning signs of emotional upset; crisis intervention techniques; referral criteria, counseling limits, referral resources and consultation opportunities.

Consultants

The mental health consultants selected and assigned to the geographic divisions would also undergo training. During their two-month orientation period a police familiarization format would be developed by the division commander and his staff to include such things as riding in patrol cars, attending roll calls, touring Department facilities, and other basic learning experiences. It is recognized that in order to function effectively the consultant will have to be knowledgeable about police functions and sympathetic to the goals of police work. During the orientation period the consultant would primarily be learning and would not assume his full consultant role status until both he and the division commander agreed that his background was sufficient. Subsesquently, the consultant would spend at least two hours per week at the division.

Coordination and Control

It is imperative that this program be well-coordinated and that control rest within the Department. Therefore, an important part of the consultation program would be ongoing biweekly meetings of the Department psychologist, the psychiatric consultant and concerned police administration in order to coordinate the various activities at the division level and to maintain integrity of philosophy and program within the Department.

Because the success of the consultant portion of the program will largely depend on the personalities and relationships of the concerned participants, it is important that should personality conflicts or negative criticisms develop, these be brought immediately to the attention of the program coordinators. If necessary, a consultant can be replaced if he has difficulty relating to the unit in which he is working or to the overall aims of the Department.

An important factor in obtaining unbiased results of this program will be the way in which it is presented and implemented. Administrators and division commanders would be in on the planning and operation of the project to enhance involvement and reduce negative preconceptions which could lead to invalid conclusions.

IV. EVALUATION

It is essential to build into this program a means of assessing the effectiveness of the project's value and also to feed back information necessary for programming revision and modification. Over the year's duration of the pilot project, evaluation will be done by attitude scales and ratings covering the following program aspects:
1. Before and after measures of trainee's knowledge and attitudes.
2. Effectiveness of the training process at the academy by both staff and trainees.
3. Effectiveness of the consultants at the division level using ratings of division commander and staff as well as the consultant himself.

4. An overall evaluation of the total program by involved administrators, staff and trainees.

These measures should yield data as to the programs value to the Department and the probable cost effectiveness of wider program implementation.

V. BUDGET

No budget is being requested at this time. The program would utilize existing Department personnel and consultants paid for by the County Department of Mental Health. Any materials and equipment needed would come from existing inventories. It is likely, however, that some small expenditure of funds may be necessary for purchase of necessary psychological tests and measures to evaluate the program.

EARLY WARNING PROJECT
SIX MONTH PROGRESS REPORT

This one-year pilot project, a collaborative effort between the Los Angeles Police Department and the Los Angeles County Department of Mental Health, was begun in April 1970 in West Valley and Northeast Divisions, with Harbor Division as a control (see attached program outline for details).

Doctors Reiser and Sokol presented the twelve-hour training segment to the sergeants at Northeast and West Valley, respectively. The course was duplicated during morning and evening hours at each division to accommodate different watches. Feedback on the training sessions is as follows:

Overall Rating of Training Sessions
    Excellent — 25%
    Very good — 56.25%
    Adequate — 18.75%

Attitudes Changed
    Yes — 68.75%
    No — 31.25%

Classes Helpful
    Very — 56.25%
    Somewhat — 40.62%
    Not at all — 3.13%

Additional comments from the sergeants reveal that training areas felt to be most useful were identifications of early warning signs of disturbance, counseling techniques, referral information and understanding oneself and others. Changes suggested most frequently were lengthening of the course and more time spent discussing problems. The sergeants felt that the most helpful parts of the instruction were early warning signs, an adult approach and counseling techniques. An LACDMH psychiatric consultant was assigned to each division to act as backup and resource person to the division commander and his staff. The consultants were committed to spending at least two hours weekly at each division on a regular basis.

Feedback from the Northeast Division indicates that the consultant is being accepted by the supervisors in the Division and that so far a positive relationship is being developed. Reports from West Valley Division indicate a problem with the development of a good working relationship between consultant and supervisor. If it is determined that this is largely a personality problem of the consultant, then Doctor Sokol will take the necessary steps to have a new consultant assigned to West Valley. This is currently under investigation and should be resolved before the next project staff meeting.

There have been numerous problems in the operations of this project since its inception which could well influence the perceived value of the total program. An initial problem involved obtaining and assigning consultants from the county Mental health Department. There was considerable delay at the outset because of internal organization difficulties in that department.

An additional problem has been the change of commanding officers of both divisions because of promotion, the reassignment of many of the sergeants who had participated in the training program and the change of psychiatric consultant to the Northeast Division. These shifts of personnel have complicated the establishment of good working relationships between the consultant and members of the division staff. It has also emphasized the need for retraining of sergeants newly assigned to the divisions.

An additional problem has been the relatively small amount of time the consultants have been able to invest in their assignments at each division. Although two hours weekly was considered acceptable in the beginning, it is now felt that considerably more time is necessary in order for the consultant to be effective. Additional time would permit meeting with men across watches, availability for staff retraining and presence as a resource person.

Two additional problems are of a relatively minor nature and could likely be resolved with increased contact and discussion by divisions consultants and staff. The first relates to the conflict felt between the supervisor's counseling role and his disciplinary role. A second difficulty was in viewing the consultant as a treatment person rather than as a consulting resource. Again this should be worked through fairly easily as the consultant gains a clearer understanding of his own role and can communicate and reinforce this concept to the division staff.

Initially the overall reactions to the program were mainly positive. Division commanders, supervisors and consultants all felt that the program yielded desirable benefits. However, the dislocation caused by transfers of commanders and other personnel and the change in one of the consultants, seemed to lead to some feelings of uncertainty and a loss in continuity. The current status seems to be that the program is still highly regarded in Northeast Division but that there is some doubt in West Valley Division because of the difficulty in establishing a good working relationship with the psychiatric consultant there.

The two program coordinators, Doctors Reiser and Sokol, feel that the program has considereable merit but that some modifications would be necessary in order to increase its effectiveness. One would be planning for additional training reinforcements for the supervisors at periodic intervals beyond the initial training period. This would be most feasible by shifting the training to the sergeants' school at the police academy. Here the training could be given routinely to all supervisors going through the school, thus eliminating the problem of sergeants transferred out of the participating divisions and the need for constant retraining. Additional reinforcement training could also be scheduled for these sergeants at the time they take the initial segment. Another suggestion would be increasing the psychiatric consultant time at each division to about six hours instead of two. This seems to be more realistic in terms of the need for involvement in division activities and availability as a resource person.

It seems highly desirable to consider the feasibility of a grant proposal to fund this program on a Department-wide basis in order to get a better measure of its effectiveness. A more sophisticated evaluation procedure would be possible under this approach since larger samples would be tapped. A grant would also allow us better selection of consultant personnel and would be cheaper in allowing us to hire and control our own staff people rather than relying on the largesse of a somewhat unreliable outside agency. It is estimated that five half-time professional consultants could be hired under a grant to consult in all geographical divisions and to do the teaching at the sergeants' school at the academy. An evaluation psychologist and a clerical person could also be hired to perform a comprehensive evaluation. The tentative estimate for this grant proposal would approximate $105,000.00 per year. A request for a three-year study would seem desirable.

October 27, 1970

BIBLIOGRAPHY

1. Bower, Eli M. et al.: AMERICAN JOURNAL OF ORTHOPSYCHIATRY, 30, 1961.
2. Sokol, R. J. and Reiser, M.: Training police sergeants in early warning signs of emotional upset. MENTAL HYGIENE, pp. 303-307, July, 1971.
3. Srole, Leo et al.: Mental Health in the Metropolis: THE MIDTOWN MANHATTAN STUDY. New York, McGraw-Hill, 1962.

EARLY WARNING PILOT PROJECT
FINAL EVALUATION

The one-year Early Warning Project pilot study was completed on April 1, 1971, in West Valley and Northeast Divisions. Emphasizing primary prevention, this project trained sergeants in the early warning signs of emotional upset, brief counseling techniques and referral resources. A Los Angeles County Department of Mental Health psychiatric consultant was assigned to each division to act as backup and resource person to the division commander and his staff.

The six-month progress report included a preliminary evaluation of the project. At that time, 81 percent of the supervisors involved rated the twelve hours of classes as excellent or very good. In addition, 69 percent of the supervisors reported a change in attitude as a result of the training sessions. Sergeants felt that the most helpful areas of the training were early warning signs of emotional disturbances, use of an adult approach and counseling techniques.

The preliminary report pointed out several problems in the operation of the project. An initial problem was a delay in the assigning of the consultants from the County Mental Health Department. Shifts of personnel (commanding officers, sergeants and psychiatric consultant) complicated the establishment of good working relationships between the consultants and members of the division staff. In spite of these problems, the overall reactions to the program at the six-month point were mainly positive.

In the final evaluation, the commanding officers of both divisions gave the project the second highest rating on a five-point scale (somewhat valuable). On all dimensions both captains recommended further implementation of this kind of program.

The consultants involved rated the overall project from very valuable to somewhat valuable. The consultants felt the need for maintaining continuity of consultative contact and periodic reinforcement of training for the sergeants. Feedback from the sergeant supervisors involved in the pilot project is as follows;

SUPERVISORS' OPINION OF PROJECT'S OVERALL VALUE

	Very Valuable	Somewhat Valuable	Undecided	Of Little Value	Worthless
Supervisors who participated in original lecture series	9%	60%	9%	22%	0%
Supervisors who did not participate in original lecture series	20%	60%	0%	20%	0%
Total % all Supervisors	12%	61%	6%	21%	0%

In rating the usefulness of the project, the sergeants reported it useful to the supervisors, not too useful in the community and useful with fellow officers.

SUPERVISORS' OPINION OF PROJECT'S "USEFULNESS TO YOU"

TOTAL SAMPLE

	Very Valuable	Somewhat Valuable	Undecided	Of Little Value	Worthless
As a supervisor	12%	60%	3%	24%	0%
In the community	3%	27%	24%	45%	0%
With fellow officers	15%	42%	18%	24%	0%

Additional comments from the supervisors in regard to the training portion of the project reveals that sergeants would like fewer lectures and more discussion of individual cases. Some sergeants felt the material covered was too general. They stressed the necessity for more initial training time and additional training reinforcement.

When asked about the psychiatric consultants assigned to the project, West Valley supervisors were discontent with their original consultant but very pleased with the second consultant who completed the project. One sergeant wrote, "He was very good. He could be understood and talked at our level." Northeast Division supervisors felt their consultant was "good."

In regard to the operation of the project, supervisors pointed out the need for more frequent and regularly scheduled meetings with the consultants. Sergeants felt that consultants must understand police work and should concentrate on individual case examples. One sergeant recommended a full-time psychiatric consultant at each division, while another sergeant felt, "Our screening process picks out most of our oddballs. We are not faced with these problems."

Overall, the reactions to the program were mostly positive indicating that in spite of transfers of personnel and organizational problems, there were definite gains which participants felt should be further pursued.

In subsequent projects it is essential that project continuity be maintained in spite of personnel shifts. Consultants involved in future programs must be police oriented. More comprehensive training and consulting programming would also be helpful.

In view of the problems which had to be dealt with during the project and the cautious attitude police personnel maintain towards "outsiders" involved in police affairs, the extensive "somewhat valuable" rating given the project by all concerned leads to the conclusion that the Early Warning Project was successful.

May 12, 1971

Appendix IV

MARITAL SURVEY (A SAMPLE)

INTRODUCTION

FOR a number of years rumor has been perpetuated to the effect that policemen have the highest divorce rate of any occupational group and specifically, that the Los Angeles Police Department divorce rate has been extremely high. Several weeks ago a news article about the Seattle Police Department mentioned an informal survey revealing that within three years after appointment 60 percent of their men had been divorced.

Because the above figures seemed inordinately high and because substantiating data were not available either locally or at the state or national levels, a survey was initiated here to establish the facts of the matter for this Department.

PROCEDURE

Eight hundred men, over 10 percent of the total sworn personnel, were surveyed to yield a stratified sample across ranks, watches, assignments and years of experience.

Questionnaires maintaining anonymity were distributed at roll calls, classes and staff meetings. The reliability of the resultant data assumes honest responses to the questions and adequate size and representativeness of the sample.

RESULTS

Overall, the data reveal that the divorce experience for sworn personnel on the Los Angeles Police Department is comparatively low. The divorce rate for the total Los Angeles Police Department sample was 21.08 percent based on a ratio of all marriages to all divorces reported (Table I). This is in contrast to a national divorce rate of approximately 30 percent and a California divorce rate of approximately 45 percent.

Within the first three years after appointment, the Los Angeles Police

TABLE I

DIVORCE RATE

Ratio of Divorces to Marriages

Total number divorces	183
Total number marriages	868
Divorce Rate	21.08%

Overall Divorce Experience

N=800

Total divorces before appointment	4.6%
Total divorces after appointment	18.3%
Total divorce experience	22.9%

TABLE II

THREE YEAR DIVORCE EXPERIENCE

N = 800 men

Total divorces occurring within 3 years after appointment - N = 39

% Divorce experience within 3 years after appointment - 4.9%

Department divorce experience was found to be 4.9 percent as compared to the Seattle Police Department report of 60 percent (Table II). Comparing high crime rate divisions with lower crime rate divisions within the Department revealed no meaningful divorce pattern. The only difference was between 77th Street Division and Central Division — 77th Street was significantly higher — and between West Los Angeles and Central Division — West Los Angeles was significantly higher (Table IIIA).

Comparison by assignment (patrol, detectives, staff, etc.) reveals several significant differences in divorce experience. Metropolitan Division showed a significantly lower divorce experience than Traffic Enforcement Division, staff personnel and combined patrol divisions. Another significant difference revealed that Traffic Enforcement Division was higher than Accident Investigation Division in divorce experience (Table IIIB).

Comparison across ranks shows a significant drop in divorce experience in higher ranks including captain and above. No significant differences occurred

TABLE IIIA

CROSS COMPARISONS

By Patrol Division

	Total	%Divorced Before Appt.	% Separated	% Divorced After Appt.
North Hollywood	120	0	2.4	16.7%
*77th Street	68	1.5	3.0	20.6%
*Central	65	3.1	3.1	9.2%
Southwest	35	2.8	5.7	11.4%
*West Los Angeles	33	0	6.1	24.2%
Van Nuys	28	0	3.6	17.9%
Rampart	36	5.5	5.5	11.1%

*The difference between Central Division and 77th Street Division is significant at the .05 level. The difference between Central Division and West Los Angeles Division is significant at the 0.5 level.

TABLE IIIB

CROSS COMPARISONS

By Assignment

	Total	% Divorced Before Appt.	% **Separated	% Divorced After Appt.
*Staff Assignments	54	1.9	1.8	18.5%
*Traffic Enforcement	42	0	2.3	31.0%
*Accident Investigation	37	0	2.7	13.5%
*Metropolitan	47	0	0	6.4%
Detectives	33	0	3.1	15.1%
*All patrol divisions	396	1.2	3.8	18.2%
All special assignments	204	1.0	3.4	23.5%

*The difference between Traffic Enforcement Division and Accident Investigation Division is significant at the .05 level. The difference between Staff Assignments and Metropolitan Division is significant at the 0.5 level. The difference between Patrol Divisions and Metropolitan Division is significant at the .05 level. The difference between Traffic Enforcement Division and Metropolitan Division is significant at the 0.1 level.

between lower ranks (Table IIIC). When different watches were compared, the AM group showed a significantly higher divorce experience than the PM group. The day watch sample was too small to be reliable (Table IIID).

A comparison by years of experience reveals a potential divorce hazard during various career points. As indicated in Table IV, the highest divorce

TABLE IIIC

CROSS COMPARISONS

By Rank

	Total	% Divorced Before Appt.	% Separated	% Divorced After Appt.
*Patrol & Detective Bureau Commanders	52	1.9	1.9	7.7%
*Sergeants' & Juvenile Investigators' Schools	61	1.6	4.9	19.7%
Staff Policemen	54	1.9	1.8	18.5%
*Patrol Policemen	396	1.2	3.8	18.2%

*The difference between Patrol and Detective Bureau Commanders and Sergeants' and Juvenile Investigators' Schools is significant at the 0.5 level. The difference between Patrol and Detective Bureau Commanders and Patrol Policemen is significant at the 0.5 level.

TABLE IIID

CROSS COMPARISONS
By Watch

	Total	% Divorced Before Appt.	% Separated	% Divorced After Appt.
*PM	187	2.7	4.8	17.1%
*AM	70	0	3.0	31.3%
Day	30	3.3	3.3	0

*The difference between PM and AM is significant at the 0.5 level.

hazard occurs during the first three years and the second highest during the six-to-ten year period. Otherwise, there is a steadily decreasing divorce probability over time on the job.

An interesting sidelight revealed by the data is the current trend toward divorce earlier in one's marriage. Three times as many policemen are currently divorced prior to appointment compared to those appointed five years ago. This trend toward early divorce may represent changes in values from those of the past wherein people hesitated longer before divorcing.

The rumor about the high divorce experience among Los Angeles policemen was not substantiated by this survey. To the contrary, divorce experience on the Los Angeles Police Department is significantly below both the state and national averages. These findings seem consistent with numerous

TABLE IV

DIVORCE ACROSS YEARS OF EXPERIENCE

Year of Occurrence	Cumulative Total % of Men Divorced to that Time	% of Total Divorces Occurred After Appt. During Years Indicated	Potential Divorce Hazard During Years Ranked from Highest Lowest
1 - 3	4.9%	26.7%	1
4 - 5	8.6%	19.8%	3
6 - 10	12.9%	23.9%	2
11 - 15	14.0%	6.2%	4
16 - 20	14.6%	3.4%	5
20+	15.1%	2.7%	6
Unknown	18.3%	17.1%	

research studies which conclude that police populations are above average both intellectually and in emotional stability.

June 22, 1971

ADDITIONAL BIBLIOGRAPHY

1. Aaron, James E. & Shafter, Albert: THE POLICE OFFICER AND ALCOHOLISM. Springfield, Thomas, 1963.
2. Adorno, T. W. et. al.: THE AUTHORITARIAN PERSONALITY. New York, Harper, 1950.
3. Allport, Gordon: THE NATURE OF PREJUDICE. Garden City, Doubleday, 1954.
4. Barth, Alan: LAW ENFORCEMENT VERSUS THE LAW. Riverside, Collier, 1963.
5. Becker, H.: OUTSIDERS: STUDIES IN THE SOCIOLOGY OF DEVIANCE. New York, Free Press, 1963.
6. Becker, H. & Felkenes, G.: LAW ENFORCEMENT – A SELECTED BIBLIOGRAPHY. New York, Scarecrow, 1968.
7. Bendix, R.: WORK AND AUTHORITY IN INDUSTRY. New York, Harper, 1963.
8. Bettleheim, B. & Janowitz, M.: SOCIAL CHANGES AND PREJUDICE. New York, Free Press, 1964.
9. Bittner, Egon: THE FUNCTIONS OF THE POLICE IN MODERN SOCIETY. National Institute of Mental Health, November 1970.
10. Blau, P.: THE DYNAMICS OF BUREAUCRACY. Chicago, 1955.
11. Bradford, L., Gelb, J. & Benne, K.: T-GROUP THEORY AND LABORATORY METHOD. New York, Wiley, 1964.
12. Brown, C.: MANCHILD IN THE PROMISED LAND. New York, Macmillan, 1966.
13. Cartwright, D.& Zander, A.: GROUP DYNAMICS. New York, Row, Peterson and Co., 1953.
14. Clark, K.: DARK GHETTO: DILEMMAS OF SOCIAL POWER, New York, Harper, 1965.
15. Cleaver, E.: SOUL ON ICE. New York, McGraw, 1968.
16. Cloward, R. & Ohlin, L.: DELINQUENCY AND OPPORTUNITY: A THEORY OF DELINQUENT GANGS. New York, Free Press, 1960.
17. Conot, R.: RIVERS OF BLOOD, YEARS OF DARKNESS. New York, Bantam, 1967.
18. Curry, J. E. & King, G. D.: RACE TENSIONS AND THE POLICE. Springfield, Thomas, 1962.

19. Dressler, D.: THE PRACTICE AND THEORY OF PROBATION AND PAROLE. New York, Columbia, 1959.
20. Dudycha, G.: PSYCHOLOGY FOR LAW ENFORCEMENT OFFICERS. Springfield, Thomas, 1960.
21. Durkheim, E.: PROFESSIONAL ETHICS AND CIVIL MORALS. Routledge & Kegan Paul, 1957.
22. Eissler, K.: SEARCHLIGHTS ON DELINQUENCY. New York, International, 1949.
23. Feuer, L.: THE CONFLICT OF GENERATIONS, New York, Basic Books, 1968.
24. Flugel, J. C.: MAN, MORALS AND SOCIETY. New York, International, 1945.
25. Fuller, L.: THE MORALITY OF LAW. New Haven, Yale, 1964.
26. Grant, J.: BLACK PROTEST. Greenwich, Fawcett, 1968.
27. Grier, W. & Cobbs, P.: BLACK RAGE. New York, Basic Books, 1968.
28. Griffin, J.: STATISTICS ESSENTIAL FOR POLICE EFFICIENCY. Springfield, Thomas, 1958.
29. Goffman, E.: STIGMA: NOTES ON THE MANAGEMENT OF SPOILED IDENTITY. Englewood Cliffs, Prentice-Hall, 1963.
30. Hart, H. L. A.: LAW, LIBERTY AND MORALITY. Stanford, Stanford, 1963.
31. Hewitt, C. P.: THE POLICE AND THE PUBLIC. New York, James, Heineman, 1962.
32. Hoch, P. & Zubra, J.: PSYCHIATRY AND THE LAW. Grune, 1955.
33. Holcomb, R. L.: THE POLICE AND THE PUBLIC. Springfield, Thomas, 1959.
34. Homans, G.: THE HUMAN GROUP. New York, Harcourt, 1950.
35. Jencks, C. & Riesman, D.: THE ACADEMIC REVOLUTION. Garden City, Doubleday, 1968.
36. Karpman, B.: THE SEXUAL OFFENDER AND HIS OFFENSE. New York, Julian 1954.
37. Keve, P.: PRISON, PROBATION OR PAROLE. Minneapolis, U. of Minn. 1954.
38. Klineberg, O.: SOCIAL PSYCHOLOGY, New York Holt, Rinehart and Winston, 1940.
39. La Fave, W.: ARREST: THE DECISION TO TAKE A SUSPECT INTO CUSTODY. Boston, Little, 1965.
40. Lindesmith, A. R.: THE ADDICT AND THE LAW. Bloomington, Indiana, 1965.
41. MacDonald, J. M.: HOMICIDAL THREATS. Springfield, Thomas, 1968.
42. Malcolm X.: THE AUTOBIOGRAPHY OF MALCOLM X. New York,

Grove, 1966.
43. Marrow, A., Bowers, D. & Seashore, S.: MANAGEMENT BY PARTICIPATION. New York, Harper, 1967.
44. Melnicoe, W. & Mennig, J.: ELEMENTS OF POLICE SUPERVISION. New York, Glencoe, 1969.
45. Momboisse, R. M.: COMMUNITY RELATIONS AND CRIME PREVENTION. Springfield, Thomas, 1967.
46. Parker, W.: PARKER ON POLICE. Springfield, Thomas, 1957.
47. Rapaport, A. & Chemmak, A.: PRISONER'S DILEMMAS: A STUDY IN CONFLICT AND COOPERATION. Ann Arbor, U. of Mich., 1965.
48. Redl, F. & Wineman, D.: CHILDREN WHO HATE. New York, Free Press, 1951.
49. Rokeach, M.: THE OPEN AND THE CLOSED MIND. New York, Basic Books, 1960.
50. Rokeach, M.: BELIEFS, ATTITUDES AND VALUES. San Francisco, Jossey-Bass, 1968.
51. Runkle, P.: THE LAW UNTO THEMSELVES. Planarian Press, 1970.
52. Schien, E. & Bennes, W.: PERSONAL AND ORGANIZATIONAL CHANGE THROUGH GROUP METHODS. New York, Wiley, 1965.
53. Sellin, T. & Wolfgang, M.: THE MEASUREMENT OF DELINQUENCY. New York, Wiley, 1964.
54. Sawle, C. R. (Ed.): POLICE POWER AND INDIVIDUAL FREEDOM. Chicago, Aldine, 1962.
55. Toch, H.: VIOLENT MEN. Chicago, Aldine, 1969.
56. Towler, J. E.: THE POLICE ROLE IN RACIAL CONFLICT. Springfield, Thomas, 1964.
57. West D. J.: THE YOUNG OFFENDERS. New York, Int. Univs., 1967.
58. Whitaker, B.: THE POLICE. Baltimore, Penguin, 1964.
59. Wiener, N.: CYBERNETICS. Cambridge, M.I.T., 1961.
60. Wilson, O. W.: POLICE PLANNING, 2nd ed. Springfield, Thomas, 1958.
61. Witmer, H. & Kotensky, R.: NEW PERSPECTIVES FOR RESEARCH IN JUVENILE DELINQUENCY. U. S. Children's Bureau Publication #356, 1956.
62. Winters, J. E.: CRIME AND KIDS – A POLICE APPROACH TO THE PREVENTION AND CONTROL OF JUVENILE DELINQUENCY. Springfield, Thomas, 1959.
63. Wolfgang, M. E.: CRIME AND RACE. Institute of Human Relations Press, 1964.

AUTHOR INDEX

Aaron, James E., 107
Abbatiello, A., 31
Ackhoff, Russell, 15
Adorno, T. W., 107
Allport, Gordon, 107
Amir, Yehuda, 31
Arther, Richard, 54

Bach, George, 25
Baehr, Melany, 31, 58, 62
Banton, Michael, 10
Bard, M., 36, 45, 58, 63
Barth, Alan, 107
Becker, Harold, 10, 107
Bendix, R., 107
Benne, K., 107
Bennes, W., 109
Berne, Eric, 25
Bettleheim, B., 107
Bittner, Egon, 107
Blau, P., 107
Blum, R., 27, 31
Blumstein, A., 63
Bordua, David, 10
Bower, Eli M., 98
Bowers, D., 109
Bradford, L., 107
Brandstatter, A. F., 46
Briggs, L. J., 46
Brown, C., 107
Buckley, W., 63

Camps, F. E., 54
Caplan, G., 50
Cartwright, D., 107
Chemmak, A., 109
Chevigny, Paul, 10
Clark, K., 107
Clark, Ramsey, 10
Cleaver, E., 107
Cleveland, S. E., 64

Clor, Henry, 54
Cloward, R., 107
Coates, Joseph, 54
Cobbs, P., 108
Conot, R., 107
Cook, R., 63
Cressey, Donald, 54
Curry, J. E., 107

Davidson, Henry, 54
Dieckmann, Edward, 54
Doig, Jameson W., 22, 25, 63
Dressler, D., 108
Drucker, Peter, 15, 46, 50, 69
Dudycha, G. J., 46, 108
Due, Lloyd, 31
Durkheim, E., 108

Eissler, K., 108
Epstein, C., 46

Fairweather, G. W., 63
Felkenes, George, 10, 107
Ferracuti, Franco, 55
Feuer, L., 108
Flugel, J. C., 108
Fuller, L., 108

Gammage, A. Z., 46
Gelb, J., 107
Gilbert, R., 47, 50
Glaser, E. M., 58, 63
Goffman, E., 108
Goffman, Irving, 15, 50
Goldstein, Leo, 31
Gottesman, Jay, 31
Grant, J., 108
Grier, W., 108
Griffin, J., 108

Halleck, Seymour, 54

Hankey, Richard, 31
Hart, H. L. A., 108
Hewitt, C. P., 108
Hoch, P., 108
Hodges, Allen, 68, 69
Hoffer, A., 54
Hogan, Robert, 32
Holcomb, R. L., 108
Hollister, Leo, 54
Homans, G., 108

Iannone, N., 46

Janowitz, M., 107
Jencks, C., 108
Johansson, Charles, 32

Karpman, Benjamin, 54, 108
Keniston, K., 63, 73
Kerlinger, F., 63
Keve, P., 108
King, G. D., 107
Klineberg, O., 108
Kling, S., 54
Kotensky, R., 109

La Fave, W., 108
Levinson, H., 46, 48, 50
Levy, Ruth, 32, 63
Lindesmith, A. R., 108

MacDonald, J. M., 108
Mahendy, William, 54
Malcolm X, 108
Marris, P., 63
Marrow, A., 109
Matarazzo, J., 32
Matson, Floyd, 15
McDonald, John M., 54
McManus, George, 32
Melnicoe, W., 109
Mennig, J., 109
Menninger, Karl, 11, 21, 25, 50, 54
Mills, Robert B., 32
Missildine, W. Hugh, 17, 25
Momboisse, R. M., 109
Montague, Ashley, 15

Neff, W., 50

Newman, L. E., 63
Niederhoffer, Arthur, 20, 25

Odiorne, George, 15
Ohlin, L., 107
Oppenheim, A. N., 63
Osmond, H., 54

Packer, Herbert, 11, 25
Parker, W., 109
Petersen, Margaret, 32

Radelet, L. A., 46
Rankin, James, 32
Rapaport, A., 109
Reddin, T., 63
Redl, F., 109
Rein, M., 63
Reiser, M., 5, 11, 25, 50, 63, 64, 89, 95, 97, 98
Reiss, Albert, 11
Reuben, David, 26
Roche, Philip, 55
Rokeach, M., 109
Runkle, P., 109

Sawle, C. R., 109
Sayles, Leonard, 15, 50
Schien, E., 109
Seashore, S., 109
Sellin, T., 109
Shafter, Albert, 107
Siegel, A., 46
Sikes, M. P., 64
Singer, H. A., 56, 64
Skolnick, Jerome, 20, 24, 26
Smith, Bruce, 11
Sokol, Robert, 60, 64, 89, 95, 97, 98
Srole, Leo, 98
Steinberg, J. L., 58, 63
Storr, Anthony, 23, 26
Strauss, George, 15, 50
Sullivan, Eugene, 32

Thorwald, Jurgen, 55
Toch, H., 109
Towler, J. E., 109
Turner, William, 11

Varsos, Milton, 32
Von Bertalanffy, Ludwig, 15

Walther, Regis, 19, 20, 26, 32
Ward, David, 54
Watson, N. A., 46
Watzlawick, Paul, 15
West, D. J., 109
Whitaker, B., 109

Wiener, N., 109
Wilson, James Q., 11, 25, 26
Wilson, O. W., 109
Witmer, H., 109
Wineman, D., 109
Winters, J. E., 109
Wolfgang, Marvin E., 55, 109

Zander, A., 107
Zubra, J., 109

SUBJECT INDEX

A

Acting out, 65
Adolescents, 24
Aggression, 23
Applied research, 58
   see also Research
Assessment, 52
Assistant chiefs, 43
Attitudes 13, 82
   a cynical attitude, 82
   ethnocentrism, 83
   prejudice, 83
   stereotyping, 83
   superior attitude, 84
   see also Objectivity
Authoritarian personality, 20
Authority, 25
Authority figures, 9, 24

B

Background investigation, 28
Basic Car Plan, 34, 59, 81
Beck, George E., ix
Behavioral Science Resource Committee, 15, 61
Behavioral scientist, 68
Biases, 9
Board of Rights, 53, 66
Brainwashed, 48
Brennan, Charles E., ix
Budget, 95
Bureau of Social Science Research, 57
Burk Foundation for Education, 58

C

Captains, 33
Career development, 30
Case reports, 34

Certification, 29
Change agent, 49
Chicago Police Department, 28, 58
Chief of Police, 43
Civil service tests, 28
Clinical psychologist, 66
Clinical skills, 53
Closed circuit television, 44
Cognitive approaches, 60
Communication, 13, 62
   see also Problems of communication
Communication system, 44
Community orientation, 34
Community relations, 51
Complaints, 13
Complementary projection, 25
Confidential, 18, 66
Confidentiality, 48, 65
   see also Limits of confidentiality
Confidential relationship, 16
Conflict areas, 13
Coordinator, 14
Counseling, 16
   conjoint marital, 16
   family, 16
   group, 16
   individual, 16
   time-limited, 17
   see also Counseling role
Counseling limits, 61
Counseling role, 39
   confrontation, 42
   counseling, 41
   limits, 42
   listening, 41
   personal problems, 40
   prejudging, 42
   psychological distance, 42
   supervisor, 39, 41
   ventilation, 41
   warning signs, 40

Subject Index

Counseling techniques, 92
Constructive arguing, 17
Consultant, 33, 48, 49
Consultant function, 47
Consultation, 15, 70, 92
Consulting firm, 58
Criminal activity, 65
Criminals, 24
Crisis, 17
Crisis intervention, 60
   techniques, 61, 93
Criteria, 29
Critical incident techniques, 34
Culture-free tests, 30
Cutting scores, 28

D

Danger and authority, 20
Dangerous situations, 37
Davis, Chief Edward M., v, 82
Delinquents, 24
Developments, 72
Diagnosis, 17
Direct services, 66, 70
Divorce experience, 104
   see also Projects

E

ESP, 12
Economic, 36
Education, 27
Emotional stability, 21, 27
Emotionally unstable, 30
Encounter group, 34
Ethical principles, 65
Evaluation, 17, 61, 94
Executive stresses, 45
   image, 45
   status quo, 45
Expert witness, 52

F

Familiarization, 8, 62
Families, 13
Family counseling, 65
   see also Counseling

Family disputes, 35, 59
Family service, 36
Feedback, 44, 47
Films, 34
Final evaluation, 98

G

Game playing, 17
Gates, Daryl F., ix
Generalist, 13
Goals, 45
Good administrator, the, 39
   participation, 39
   self-motivation, 39
Grant, 57
Grant proposal, 59
Grantsmanship, 60
Growth, 70

H

Handbook, 34
Harbor Division, 95
Hardware, 72
Hierarchy, 44
High speed pursuits, 60
Homicidal, 42
   see also Referral
Homicides, 52
Hospitalization, 43
Houston, 58
Hoy, Vernon L., ix
Human relations, 33, 58
Human Relations Handbook, 77
   see also Projects
Human side, 56
Human values, 72

I

Identification, 47
   see also Objectivity
Identity, 27
In-house, 16
In-house psychologist, 3
In-house research, 61
"in" member, 12
Instrumentation, 58

Integrity, 27
Intelligence, 21, 27, 53
Internal affairs, 53
International Association of Chiefs of Police, 29, 60
Item analysis, 52

J

JAIM, 20
Job-related, 16
JOURNAL OF CRIMINAL LAW, CRIMINOLOGY AND LAW ENFORCEMENT, 8
Juvenile delinquency, 33

L

LAW AND ORDER RECONSIDERED, 10
LEAA, 57
Learning systems, 33
Legal, 36
Lieutenants, 33
Limits of confidentiality, 65
Line-staff, 14
Los Angeles County Department of Mental Health, 60, 89, 91, 95
Los Angeles Police Academy, 58
Los Angeles Police Department, 28, 29, 34, 36, 40, 59, 60, 70, 75, 81, 84, 89, 95, 101, 104
Loyalty, 48

M

Mace, 23
Magical powers, 48, 68
Managers, 48, 68
Manliness, 66
Manual, 7
Marital, 65
Marital problems, 16
Marital survey, 101
Masculinity, 87
  see also Self-image
Mechanical-technical, 56
Medical aid, 36
Mental health agencies, 14
Mental health consultants, 60, 93

Mentally ill, 33, 35
  see also Projects
Mexican-American, 81
Miami Police Department, 57
Middle management, 13, 38
Minority groups, 24
Model, 59

N

National commission, 56
National Research Institute, 57
Negro, 81
New York Police Department, 36
Non-verbal communication, 51
Northeast Division, 95

O

Objectivity, 67
  attitudes, 67
  identification, 67
  pressure to conform, 67
  shaping influences, 67
  unconscious need, 67
Occupational personalities, 19, 20
Omnibus Crime Control and Safe Streets Act, 57
On-the-scene assistance, 53
  campus disturbance, 54
  crowd confrontation, 54
  mentally disturbed, 54
Oral board, 28
Oriental, 81
Orientation, 7, 62

P

Parker, William H., 80, 81
Patrol, 8, 13, 70
Peace Officers Standards and Training Commission, 29, 60
Performance criteria, 27
Personal, 16
Personal adaptability, 48
Personal attributes, 69
Personal characteristics, 4
Personality, 57
Physical examination, 28

POLICE, 8
POLICE CHIEF, 8
Police-community relations, 25
Police personality, 81
Police psychologist, 4
Police selection, 58
Policeman's role, 80
Pornography, 52
　see also Projects
President's Commission on Law Enforcement and the Administration of Justice, 57, 62, 80, 81
Prevention, 72
Primary prevention, 57, 60, 72, 89, 91
Privileged, 65
Problems, 8, 61, 96
　job related, 19
　personality development, 19
　traumatic situations, 19
Problems of anger and provocation, 86
　being manipulated, 86
　policemen as authority symbol, 86
Problems of communication, 84
　discourtesy, 84
　excessive familiarity, 84
　name-calling, 84
　nonverbal communication, 85
　not explaining actions, 85
　not listening, 85
　overseriousness, 86
　profanity, 84
Problems of policemen, 19
Professional policeman, 87
Progress report, 95
Projection, 24
Projects, 75
　career guidance, 75
　counseling principles, 75
　decision-making, 75
　divorce experience, 76
　driver training program, 75
　expert witness, 76
　homicidal behavior, 75
　human relations handbook, 76
　I.Q. needs, 75
　mentally ill, 75
　murders, 75
　pilot project, 75
　pornography, 76

　research, 75
　secondary schools, 75
　shooting, 75
　stress, 75
　suicidal, 75
Promotion, 29
Psychiatric standards, 28
Psychiatry, 37
Psychological predictors, 59
Psychological services, 70
Psychological services division, 31
Psychological tests, 29
　California Psychological Inventory, 29
　California Test of Mental Maturity, 29
　MMPI, 29
Psychological testing, 28
　Group Rorschach, 28
　Minnesota Multiphasic Personality Inventory, 28
　Tree Drawing, 28
Psychosomatic illnesses, 37
Psychotherapy, 16
Psychotic behavior, 12
　see also Referral
Public relations, 9
　interviews, 9
　meetings, 9
　panels, 9
　radio, 9
　talks, 9
　television program, 9
Puerto Rican, 81

Q

Qualifications, 4
Questionnaire design, 52

R

Rating scales, 61
Rationale, 3
Recruit, 66
Recruit training, 33
Redondo Beach, Calif. Police Department, 58
Referral, 42
　financial problems, 42
　homicidal, 42

making a, 43
psychotic behavior, 42
suicidal, 42
Referral resources, 18, 61, 92
Related agencies, 13
Relationship, 65
Representative, 14
Research, 56, 58, 70
  see also In-house research, projects
Research design, 60
Research project, 89
Retesting, 31
Role, 47
Role expectations, 69
Role playing, 34

S

Sampling techniques, 51
San Francisco State College, 58
San Mateo, 58
Scapegoat, 24
Scapegoating, 10, 49
Seattle Police Department, 101
Selection, 5, 12, 29
Selection and training, 93
Self-image, 17, 36, 37
  masculinity, 36, 37
Sensitivity training, 34, 52
Sergeants, 33, 61, 92, 93
Sergeants' class, 66
Service function, 21
Sex, 23
Sex offenses, 33
Sexuality, 17
Shootings, 60
  see also Projects
Simulation, 60
Skills, 4
Small group discussions, 34, 51, 58
Social change, 22
Specialized assignments, 31
Speck, Dale H., ix
Staff responsibilities, 18
Staff role, 12, 66
Standardization, 29
Statistical precision, 59
Status, 12
Status quo, 22, 68

  see also Executive stresses
Stereotype, 24, 68
Stereotypes, 51
Stereotyped, 4
Stereotyping, 34, 49
  see also Attitudes
Stratified random sample, 51
Stress, 38, 57
  see also Projects
Stress occupation, 16
Stresses, 37
  see also Executive stresses
Suicidal, 35, 65
  see also Projects, referral
Supervisors, 13
  see also Counseling role
Surveys, 51
Suspiciousness, 21, 62, 67
Symbols, 34

T

Taboos, 23
The Task Force Report on Police, 5, 59
Teacher, 33
Teaching techniques, 33
Through channels referral, 18
Top management, 43, 45
  ambivalence, 44
  conflicts, 44
  unconsciously, 44
Training, 70
Training officers, 35
Training programs, 33

U

Unconscious processes, 51
Unconsciously, 68
  see also Top management
Universities, 14

V

Vice, 52
Videotape feedback, 34
Vocational, 36
Vocational guidance, 30
Vocational psychologist, 31

W

Washington, D. C. Department of Corrections, 57

West Valley, 95
Wickersham Commission, 3, 5, 57
Wives, 37
Writing, 13